MASTERY

MASTERY

How Learning Transforms Our Brains,
Minds, and Bodies

ARTURO E. HERNANDEZ, PhD

Prometheus Books

Essex, Connecticut

Prometheus Books

An imprint of Globe Pequot, the trade division of
The Rowman & Littlefield Publishing Group, Inc.
4501 Forbes Blvd., Ste. 200
Lanham, MD 20706
www.rowman.com

Distributed by NATIONAL BOOK NETWORK

British Library Cataloguing in Publication Information Available

Library of Congress Cataloging-in-Publication Data

Names: Hernandez, Arturo E., author.
Title: Mastery : how learning transforms our brains, minds, and bodies /
  Arturo E. Hernandez, PhD.
Description: Lanham : Prometheus Books, [2024] | Includes bibliographical
  references and index. | Summary: "For anyone looking to learn a new
  skill, teach someone else to do the same, or to better understand how
  our brains evolve and excel, this fascinating tour of cognition will
  reveal the path to surprising potential"— Provided by publisher.
Identifiers: LCCN 2023036311 (print) | LCCN 2023036312 (ebook) | ISBN
  9781633889408 (cloth ; alk. paper) | ISBN 9781633889415 (epub)
Subjects: LCSH: Learning, Psychology of. | Ability. | Cognition. |
  Learning—Physiological aspects.
Classification: LCC BF318 .H47 2024 (print) | LCC BF318 (ebook) | DDC
  153.1/5—dc23/eng/20231127
LC record available at https://lccn.loc.gov/2023036311
LC ebook record available at https://lccn.loc.gov/2023036312

∞™ The paper used in this publication meets the minimum requirements of
American National Standard for Information Sciences—Permanence of Paper
for Printed Library Materials, ANSI/NISO Z39.48-1992.

CONTENTS

PREFACE

The idea that we use only one language for all that we do is completely foreign to me. I was born in the late 1960s in Berkeley, California, into a family that was Spanish speaking. I spent the majority of my childhood and adolescence ping-ponging between Mexico and the United States. Summers and the holiday seasons were spent with extended family in Mexico. When I was in the ninth grade, my parents sent me to study for a year in Mexico. It was full immersion for a whole year. This immersion led to full literacy as my Spanish skills erupted as I took all my classes in a language that I had always spoken but rarely read.

As I came back to the United States to finish high school and then spent the first two years of college in the United States, I settled back into schooling in English. Since I had spoken both languages since I was young, to me it felt like both had a symbiotic relationship. I had navigated both of them in clearly defined contexts, one used in Mexico, the other in the United States.

I also grew up in a household filled with music. My mother's family had always loved music. My mother and many of my uncles had pursued music with passion. I fell right in line. As a child, I loved all kinds of different artists. My musical interests ranged from Mexican *rancheras* and *boleros* up to Earth, Wind & Fire, Johnny Cash, and later in the 1980s, REO Speedwagon, Journey, and the Gap Band. Even pop music today has its allure. More recently, one group that has captured my imagination is Maroon 5 and its lead singer Adam Levine.

The allure of music also had unintended consequences. My dad had introduced me to Brazilian music when I was young. I grew to love it so much that it led me to want to study in Brazil for my year abroad. When I got to UC Berkeley, the week before I started my first year, I went to the Education Abroad Office. I looked at the exchange program in Brazil and read about São Paulo, Brazil's economic capital. I imagined that it would be like a Portuguese-speaking Mexico City, noisy, full of traffic, teeming with life, and full of music.

In my first year of college, I began taking Portuguese classes. At first, I had a pretty thick accent, and my understanding of Portuguese was limited. I remember that my classmates could actually speak and understand what the professor was saying. Many had outright conversations and would do their homework by talking in Portuguese. I felt like I was behind everyone. Across semesters, I kept making progress but could not catch up to my classmates.

Because I knew Spanish and had taken some Portuguese, I met the prerequisites for studying abroad in Brazil. I boarded the plane and landed ten hours later in a completely different land. It was July, warm in Los Angeles, where I had taken off. São Paulo was in the middle of winter, and the cold chilled me to the bone. The city I thought would be like Mexico City felt different. Bigger and noisier. And my Portuguese was good but slow and halting.

Then came an experience like no other I had ever had. Being immersed in Portuguese was like putting a sledgehammer to my language system. As a two-year-old, I had been exposed to Farsi for a year in home care. Even though my mom said I spoke to my caretaker, that language just kind of came and went. I was so young

I have no memory of knowing Farsi. Spanish had grown stronger as it built on all my experiences during the summers I spent in Mexico. And my year in ninth grade. However, arriving in Brazil and being immersed in Portuguese was completely different.

Portuguese tried to take over. Before I knew it, I could not say simple words in Spanish, and my English kept getting worse and worse. I ended up spending two years there, one in the exchange program and a second in a gap year that I took before completing college. During this time my proficiency in Portuguese got so good that I could pass for a native speaker.

Sounding like a native in Portuguese came at a price. When I came back to the United States at age twenty-two, everyone kept wondering what had happened to my English. My Spanish had also taken a hit. My grandmother said I had lost my beautiful Mexican accent and I spoke *muy raro*. Reading in English was slow and effortful.

By the time I finished college two years later, I had finally regained my English skills, and my Spanish had recovered. The rest of my twenties ended up being a period of language stability. Portuguese was kept around by the few times I could use it with friends or people I would meet and the songs I would occasionally sing aloud. I pretty much thought that I would remain trilingual for the rest of my life.

My language stability changed in my mid-thirties when I was invited to spend time at the Max Planck Institute in Leipzig, Germany. Going to Germany was disorienting. My mismatch with the language context in Leipzig became most apparent to me one night when I decided to hail a taxi. As I got in, I searched desperately for any way to communicate with the driver. I asked, "English?" The driver responded, *"Nein, Russisch."*

The former East Germany as part of the Soviet bloc taught its children Russian as a second language. The taxi driver and I spoke at least five languages between the two of us. But none of them in common. I handed the driver a small piece of paper with an address, he nodded, and then we drove off. As we wound through the streets, I could not help but notice the billboards. Since English and German share most of the alphabet, I could read all the words that zoomed by as we sped through the city. But it looked funny to me at that time. There were a lot of *k*'s, and some vowels had dots above them. I had no idea what all of it meant. I remember staring up at one particular billboard on a building and thinking, "This language is incomprehensible. There is no way I will ever learn to speak, read, or write it."

As was the case when I studied Portuguese, in my German classes I again felt that everyone spoke better than I did. I spent years working on my vocabulary, practicing aloud in my car, reading magazines for German adult learners, and I even went back to spend a year, and later I went for three consecutive summers. After seven years of classes, one year, and three summers, I still felt like I could not do anything spontaneously.

In 2015, fourteen years after my first visit, I was able to go back for a year and take my family with me on another research visit. The first three months of that visit were a tongue-tied form of torture. My speech was halting and slow. Group conversations were impossible. The thoughts would come in floods, but the words rolled off my tongue like mud slithering down a slide. Trips to any non-German–speaking country invariably led to all kinds of electrical cobwebs ganging up against my growing ability in German.

Suddenly, six months in, my German got much better. When people asked why my German was so good, I would reply, *"Ich habe gelittet."* I have suffered. That is the only way to describe what it was like to learn German. It was hard, with lots of ups and downs, and even today with all that work and time it is less than perfect. Then a German would invariably quote Mark Twain: "Life is too short to learn German."

During my life, I have been exposed to six different languages and gained fluency in four of them. Each of these language-learning episodes has taught me how flexible our language system is. They have taught me how the ways in which we learn change with age but also how they seem to pile up on top of one another. My Farsi might be seemingly gone, but it has to have played a role in giving me the flexibility needed to learn more than one language. My Portuguese eventually became accentless, and my German accent is very light, relatively speaking. It is almost as if all the cobwebs and back-and-forth of having to pry open my language system over time strengthened my language muscles.

All these experiences eventually led me to actually study how the brain adapts to learning more than one language. In writing my first book, *The Bilingual Brain*, I realized that learning new languages doesn't just tell us about language learning. Learning new languages also tells us about how we learn.

My work and my own experiences had yielded insights into this process of learning in general. We take what we know, we tweak it a bit, we try again, we tweak again, and so on and so forth. At times we show sudden improvement and then sudden loss. What I have come to realize is that language that in the words of Elizabeth Bates is "a new machine built out of old parts" is true of most higher-level skills that we acquire.

In *The Bilingual Brain*, I talk about languages like species in an ecosystem: at times they fight for resources, other times they cooperate, and over time they become symbiotic. As I learned more languages, each language shifted and adapted as the others came in. With all these languages in my head, my English became better in my thirties and forties, not in spite of the other languages I learned, but because of all those other languages. In my work, I have come to think about English, the language that I know the best, as having pieces of German, Spanish, and Portuguese that are sewn together.

Mastery grows naturally from my previous book. The main idea is that all the things that we marvel at as humans—language, reading, and even competitive sports—involve the combination and recombination of smaller pieces that become a greater whole. Language learning, in my mind, works as an analogy for the way in which we learn complex skills.

My childhood was not just filled with learning languages. I also did a lot of other things. Earlier I mentioned my love for music. I also loved to play sports with my friends, either in the schoolyard or in my neighborhood.

As a kid one of my favorite sports was basketball. But I never got past five feet seven, and my basketball "career" ended on the playground in middle school. I never made it far in soccer or football. That left baseball as the only game in which I played on an actual team in junior high. Hitting a baseball allowed me to discover that I had very good hand-eye coordination, which was aided by exceptional eyesight.

As I grew older, I left the schoolyard and team sports behind and took up the sport played by my family in Mexico, tennis. In tennis, I took all the sports I had learned as a child and combined them into one: throwing and catching from baseball, shooting, passing, and footwork from basketball, and throwing a football have become a collage that today I call tennis. It is as if this new sport is a chimera in which one sport is a combination of different pieces of each sport that are stitched together. The way I think about it, learning a complex skill like tennis is like learning a language. We layer together all these different experiences to create a greater whole.

The process of learning something new or becoming better at something we already know applies to everyone. Whether we are a professional in a sport, a polyglot who speaks at least eleven languages, or just learning something new and becoming good at it, the same rules apply. No matter what our ultimate level of expertise, we as humans are adept at taking a bunch of little pieces and creating a much bigger whole. Our gift as humans—our defining feature—is the emergent process that leads to mastery.

1

THE RIGHT KIND OF PRACTICE

MY DINNER WITH ANDERS

In late 2019, I was flying to Tallahassee for a scientific meeting and realized that I might have a chance to meet K. Anders Ericsson. Ericsson's ideas on deliberate practice and expertise had been the topic of almost an entire chapter in my book *The Bilingual Brain*. Even though his interests in skill learning did not appear to be perfectly aligned with my research interests, I had been intrigued by the idea that his insights might also apply to language.

Two big hobbies had come to fill my life outside of work and family as an adult: trying to become proficient in German and trying to improve my tennis game. To me there were aspects of this process that were very similar. To learn German, I would spend lots of time working on the little parts of the language—basically on hearing and repeating words, phrases, and sentences. In tennis, I would also do very much the same thing. It could be some little piece of a tennis stroke, or a movement pattern combined with a stroke. Thus, the rubric for learning could be applied to language and other motor skills in a similar way. Because of my own experiences, I had dabbled in other work that looked at the nature of expertise, looking at how college athletes differed from less skilled athletes. The trip to Tallahassee would turn out to be the perfect chance to talk to Anders about my own take on his work.

The idea to write to Anders Ericsson came to me on the first leg of my trip to Tallahassee, Florida, in December 2019. Around two o'clock in the afternoon, about an hour before I was going to land in Tampa for a short layover for my flight to Tallahassee, I jumped on the plane's Wi-Fi and emailed him with the hope that I could see him for dinner the evening before my meeting the next day. When I landed, he had already gotten back to me with a yes. He would be happy to do so. We would meet at a restaurant in downtown Tallahassee at six o'clock that night. Anders navigated the Internet to accommodate my flight delay, and when I landed in Tallahassee twenty minutes late, he had already shifted the reservation.

I approached the restaurant, and from a distance I instantly recognized the face I had seen on websites and videos as well as the numerous articles he had published. I introduced myself and we sat down. The waiter approached us and asked if we wanted anything to drink. We both hesitated, waiting for the other to order. To fill the awkward silence, the waiter wondered out loud, "Are you celebrating any special occasions? Perhaps a birthday?" I said, "As a matter of fact, yes, we are. It is not every day that I get to have dinner with one of my academic heroes." Stunned by the statement, Anders mumbled some nicety about my work.

That evening I learned a lot about Anders that I had never read in any book or article. We talked about the cornerstones of his theory, the idea that we become good at something through very specific types of practice. We also talked about the ways in which he ignored those who wanted him to publish a lot of articles. To him it was quality over quantity, one of the qualities of his work (no pun intended) that had always engendered admiration on my part.

The amazing part of my first interactions with Anders is that I expected that as a Swede he would sound like one of my tennis heroes, Björn Borg. Unlike Borg, who had a very Swedish accent, Anders had almost no accent in English. One of the things that is most resistant to improvement with age is accent. Adult learners can become seemingly accentless, but it is exceedingly rare.

I searched for reasons that might have softened his accent. For example, early language learners seem to have a much fainter accent than later learners. I asked him if he had been exposed to English at a young age. Maybe there was a teacher who was a native speaker. Maybe a parent or a friend. The answer was no. Anders had learned English in school in Sweden. His exposure to native speakers came as an adult since he spoke it at home with his family and at work with his colleagues.

The fact that Anders had learned to speak English without an accent as an adult fit in to some extent with his idea of deliberate, or deep, practice. In fact, the difference between adult and child language learners has to do with the type of interactions they have and not with the absolute age at which they started. Maybe, just maybe, in speaking with his family and friends, Ericsson had used English like a child would. And in doing that he might have lost his accent with years of intense practice. Ericsson had gone above and beyond the number of hours required to become an expert at English.

I also had my own thoughts about what might have led him to lose his accent. First, let's learn a bit more about his own views.

THE ERICSSONIAN APPROACH

K. Anders Ericsson is best known for the 10,000-hour rule, a term coined by Malcolm Gladwell in his book *Outliers*. When Gladwell looked over Ericsson's data, he proposed that it was only after 10,000 hours of practice that someone became an expert. It turns out that Ericsson never suggested that 10,000 hours was a magic number. Rather, he simply suggested that the number of hours of practice was the main determinant of how good someone was.

Ericsson's parents used one basic premise to raise him and his siblings. They told them they could do anything that wanted to. The main hitch was that achievement took a long time, leading them down a certain path. If becoming good at something was going to take a long time, it should get their attention for sustained periods of time. Ericsson's parents focused on finding topics that would interest their children and would get them hooked so that they could spend many hours improving.

One problem with tasks that take a long time to master is that there are a lot of ups and downs. How do you measure progress when success is measured in months or years and not in hours or days? To avoid putting a lot of pressure on their children to get the absolute best grades, Ericsson's parents focused on how much they kept acquiring more knowledge over time. Improvement takes effort, and that is all that was required of them. A focus on the longer road to improvement had interesting effects on Ericsson and the way that he approached learning.

Ericsson's upbringing led him to avoid using shortcuts in his own method of studying. One anecdote he tells is how he approached learning material for exams in history class. In history classes, rather than using rote memory he sought to learn the background of key figures. If he had to learn about a key battle in history, he would learn about the backgrounds of those who were involved in the battle. He would also learn about the cultural and political situation that led to the battle or to a war. The process of creating a deeper connection took longer at the beginning than simply committing a fact to memory. He noted that he almost never forgot what he had learned. Compared to his classmates, who were desperately learning and relearning the same facts over and over again, Ericsson remembered things for the test and even after he had finished the semester.

Ericsson's own experience in learning sheds light on many of the principles that emerge in his own work. His theory rests on the idea that we should use deliberate, or deep, practice, a purposeful form that breaks a larger skill down into many smaller components. This deliberate practice is similar to the approach he used in learning material slowly over time rather than just using rote memorization. We should also form mental images—what he calls *representations*—that help to capture the essence of any skill we learn. We can see this in the way he got background on the events at a particular point in time to build a mental image of a historic event.

In his view, learning was deeply mental, the product of cognitive programs that are refined over a long period of time. For K. Anders Ericsson, the road to excellence runs long and deep. This is most evident in his book *Peak*, where he argues for the importance of practice and our mental concepts as the road to excellence. In his view, almost none of the differences in human ability across individuals are due to some inborn genetic component. Outside of height and weight, Anders suggested that practice is the main determinant of a person's ultimate achievement. In fact, the very practice that people engaged in would change their biology. Even his own ability to learn English without an accent would lead us to this conclusion. His work shows us how our effort in practice and the mental images we build up along the way are what count the most toward our eventual achievement.

The mental images that are built up in our minds are called *mental representations* in the expertise literature. The idea can be thought of as re-presentation, a way of remolding the outside world so that we can access it efficiently in our minds. These images hold an important place in Ericsson's theory, as we will see next.

ON MENTAL REPRESENTATION

The importance of mental representations in experts that came to be an important part of Anders Ericsson's work can be traced back to Adriaan de Groot's dissertation on chess masters in the late 1930s. As a young adult, De Groot was a member of the Dutch national team that placed sixth and eighth in the world in two consecutive championships. He also won the Dutch National Championship in 1937 and placed fourth in 1938. After completing his degree in math and physics, he chose to pursue a doctorate in psychology, leading to a drop in his competitive chess activities. But De Groot had a hard time letting go of his passion for chess, and he began to see it as a topic of study.

His days of playing chess had filled him with various experiences that led him to look at how experts differ from less expert players. Based on his own playing, his work as a chess journalist, and discussions with Max Euwe, his teammate and chess champion, De Groot had taken a profound interest in the way that chess players think through their games. He tested some of his ideas on Euwe and with his help was able to recruit and test many of the champions at the time. He also tested less expert players to try and observe differences. Interested in this topic, he began designing studies to try to understand what was going on in players' minds.

De Groot's experiments showed that experts differed in memory especially when chessboards were shown for a few seconds. After the players looked at the boards, the pieces were removed, and the players were then asked to reconstruct the boards from memory. De Groot found a strong relationship between the number of pieces remembered and chess-playing ability. Those with higher expertise remember more pieces. Those with lower expertise remember fewer.

Better memory also helped experts make decisions quickly. Even really short glimpses at a board gave chess masters information about potential threats. An expert player could quickly figure out whether a particular layout called for an attack or for defensive maneuvers.

De Groot's dissertation work sat on the sidelines for several decades before being rekindled during a short visit he made in the 1960s to Carnegie Mellon University. During this stay, he met with Allen Newell and Herbert Simon, who were working on programming a computer to play chess. That discussion was so inspiring that when De Groot told his doctoral student Riekent Jongman about it, they quickly agreed to revive this work. Jongman would extend many of De Groot's seminal studies while completing his dissertation.

Taking advantage of new technologies, Jongman found that masters moved their eyes more smoothly and faster. They could home in on the location of a piece very quickly. The final part of Jongman's thesis looked at how master chess players used redundancy to make decisions. Specifically, Jongman found that chess masters did not see pieces individually. Rather, they saw each chess set like a pattern. Every piece was related to the other pieces and came to form what psychologists call a "chunk."

The connection between De Groot's work and the group looking into artificial intelligence at Carnegie Mellon University led to renewed interest in experiments with real chess players. Chase and Simon asked a group of players (experts versus novices) to look at chessboards and remember them. To add another wrinkle to the experiment, experts and novices were shown either possible or impossible chess layouts. Experts ended up being better than novices but only for layouts of real chess situations. If the chess pieces were placed in patterns not used in real chess games, memory in chess experts and nonexperts did not differ.

This last finding reveals something fundamental about expertise. Practice and expertise in a particular area do not rely on general aptitude. Chess masters do not have better memories and thus do not have a better memory for pieces. Their expertise is relevant for real chess layouts, not for ones they have not experienced before.

Rather than thinking about one move at a time, chess masters were seeing the game as having some form of flow across the various moves that would eventually take them to checkmate. To chess masters each move had a meaning. It's as if each move and piece became a part of a greater whole—a chunk of knowledge that could no longer be disassembled into its component parts.

THE LIMITS OF HUMAN COGNITION

Chess was not the only thing on the minds of researchers trying to understand how people became experts. Researchers were also interested in more everyday types of tasks. One task that was used extensively was a short-term memory task called a *digit span*. In this task, participants are either told or shown one digit at a time. At the end of the task, they are asked to repeat those items in the same order. These studies showed that the average span was 7 ± 2. Those at the higher range could remember nine items, and those in the lower range could remember five items.

The range in how many items people could remember led some researchers to search for reasons why this might be. H. J. Humpstone in an important article at the time declared that individual limits were most likely an inherited trait. First, people differed in the number of items they could keep in their memory. The fact that scores varied so much, even in college students, must be congenital. Second, tests with children had found that lower abilities to store items were associated with lower learning abilities. Thus, every person was born with an upper limit of items they could keep in their memory. According to Humpstone, keeping more digits in mind was not a question of practice; rather, it was handed down to us by our parents and the ability that we had at birth.

Martin and Fernberger were the first ones to question Humpstone's congenital view. They set out to test how fixed this ability

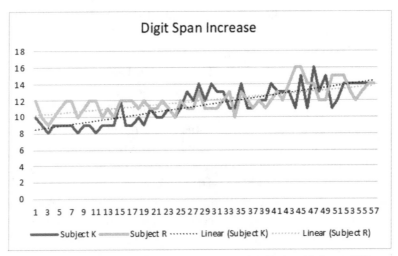

Results from training by session for subjects K and R. *Adapted from Martin and Ferberger, 1929.*

was by training two subjects, K and R, for multiple sessions on strings of digits. The results showed substantial improvement in both K and R. In the figure above, we can see the results from their study. The solid lines represent the actual scores. The dotted lines show that both K and R had scores that trended up over time. Martin and Fernberger concluded that increasing digit span is trainable and not fixed at birth.

The fact that digit span could be improved was something that also inspired Anders Ericsson. The study in 1929 had kind of fallen by the wayside. Ericsson got his chance to work more on this topic when he met Herbert Simon, a Nobel Prize–winning cognitive psychologist. Simon, as we noted earlier, had worked to revive De Groot's work on chess to create a computer program that might beat humans. He was also deeply interested in human problem-solving. To explore problem-solving, he would have people report out loud what they were thinking. It was the future Nobel Prize winner who invited Ericsson to Carnegie Mellon University in Pittsburgh to spend some time as a postdoctoral scholar.

At Carnegie Mellon, Ericsson applied the methods of verbal report used by Simon (and by De Groot years before) on a student named Steve Faloon, whom he trained one summer on remembering a long string of digits. The question Ericsson had was not whether he could train the student to remember more than eight or nine digits. The question for him was, how many more?

Ericsson was not asking the student to recall sets of numbers from his past such as phone numbers or postal codes. He was reading one digit every second, and there was not enough time for Steve to place it into long-term memory. He was asking Steve to learn new sets of numbers on the fly, and then once he learned the new one, he would have to learn another set of new ones. This would happen over and over again. Steve was exactly where he should be and no matter what he tried to do, he could not go beyond the eight or nine digits that most humans can keep in mind for a few seconds. Others had managed to remember more than that. Anders was confident that Steve would also break the nine-digit barrier.

BREAKING THROUGH THE DIGIT SPAN LIMIT

Digit span relies on short-term memory, which is limited. This leaves us as humans two options for increasing our limit. We can either increase our short-term memory or we can leverage our long-term memory by using chunking. The question remains whether a similar type of chunking strategy might work for digit span. In other words, could Steve become a digit master by leveraging his long-term memory? Or would he remain stuck in remembering each digit separately?

To overcome his limitations, Steve began to link sets of digits to a concept. Linking a fact or some new thing that has to be learned to a concept is called *mnemonics*. These memory strategies have been used for centuries to improve memory. Ancient Greek senators who did not have access to teleprompters used the method of loci. In this method, a topic is mentally placed in a room. As they practiced and learned their speeches, these senators from ancient Greece would imagine that each topic they would cover was in different parts of the chamber where they would give their speech. Anders Ericsson observed a similar approach in Chao Lu, who was able to learn Pi (3.1415 . . .) up to 67,890 digits.

Rather than using mnemonics, Steve essentially found his own strategies. He began to store four-digit and three-digit sequences as running times and ages. So, 4533135 would become 45 minutes and 33 seconds along with 13 and ½. He would then remember a marathon time and a boy going through puberty. By adding this second memory trick, Steve was able to combine both four-digit and three-digit combinations to get up to eighty digits.

The example of Steve might seem very mental in the sense that it involves taking digits and merging them with running times or ages. Researchers would call learning a very long digit string a cognitive task. The divide between mental and physical skills is not all that clear. In fact, our mental skills often take building blocks from physical actions in the world. The building up of these skills from very small pieces is a point that Anders made across his entire career, which ended when he passed away on June 17, 2020.

THE LOSS OF A HERO

At the end of our two-hour-long dinner on that December evening in 2019, Anders and I walked out of the restaurant. He approached the valet parking area and gave a young man his ticket. I could have left but decided to just stand there and keep him company. There were so many things that I felt I had not asked him about.

He offered me a ride to my hotel, and we continued conversing. As I got out of the car, I thanked him for having accepted an invitation so last minute. He told me that if I ever needed anything I should reach out to him again. I saw my own reflection in the door and the lights of his car. I turned around one last time, waved goodbye, and watched as he drove off.

In the weeks that followed, he and I exchanged a few emails on topics that had come up during our dinner. One topic that stood out was the notion that accents were very hard to lose. As I noted earlier, Anders's accent was particularly light in English, something that could fit in with the notion of deliberate practice and mental representations.

In our first email exchange, I tried to float another possibility. Maybe he had some advantage in learning a second language. I asked him if he could sing in tune. As we will see later there is a link between vocal singing and the lightness of an accent. He was not one to brag, so I was unable to figure out if he was a good singer. He did say he liked to sing. I took that as a yes. So maybe he did have an advantage in being able to sound like a native speaker.

We also discussed age of acquisition at length. One of the main points that had always seemed odd to me was how his work on expertise did not really consider when experts started to practice. The age at which we start is known to have a profound effect on how our brains manage the learning of new skills. This left a lot of unanswered questions.

How would deliberate practice and mental images change across development? After all, starting at different ages results in different end points. Most experts start young. Yet some skills can be developed later in life. Steve Falloon was able to memorize longs strings of digits by employing strategies as an adult.

I also thought a lot about biology. How does the brain figure into all of this? Are brains just hardware? Do they just work to produce neural signals that somehow turn into thoughts? If so, are the thoughts and mental representations like software? Cognitive neuroscientists think a lot about how the brain and mind are connected. How would Anders account for the biological bases of skill learning?

After two or three exchanges, my connection to Anders ran cold. The holiday season was upon us, and I wished him a nice vacation in San Diego with his family.

In the spring, on April 1, 2020, I wrote to say that I had assigned his book in my class on the bilingual brain. I commented on how his book had given me insight on tennis. Specifically, I recalled a time when an opponent had found a weakness in my game and exploited it. Challenges and moving beyond one's comfort zone are key concepts in deliberate practice. We have to practice when we are uncomfortable.

I never received a response. I assumed that he was buried in his work. A few months later I learned that he, unfortunately, had been buried in the very real sense during those weeks. I was invited to a virtual celebration of his work at Florida State University in July 2020. I am both happy and sad to have met him: Happy that I was able to at least meet him once. Sad that he left this world. I always wondered where our conversations might have led. There seemed to be so much left for us to talk about.

EMERGENCE, DEVELOPMENT, AND PRACTICE

The chapters in this book cover a lot of the topics that I might have asked Anders about. As a cognitive neuroscientist, I spend a lot of time thinking about the brain and how it relates to how we think. I am also very interested in how humans change as they go from the cradle up to adulthood and beyond. Where does a skill start and how does it change as we get older?

One of the topics we will consider in greater depth is emergence, how things combine to form something new. I'll introduce you to a concept that takes chunking a step further. When many chunks combine they can transform and become a megachunk. I will also trace out the way in which skills can be thought of as combinations of sensory and motor information. Later we will go even further and move to consider more complex parts of our brain that blend information that is and is not available to our consciousness.

Although Ericsson and I had different views on knowledge, skills, and how we acquire them, I had great admiration for the way his work had an impact on people's lives. Anders loved to work with individuals doing in-depth studies. These studies did not just consider cognitive skills like memorizing digits. They also involved physical skills like playing a sport. We now turn to one of his favorite natural experiments: the taking up of an entirely new game, golf, by an adult determined to see how far practice could take him.

2

CASE STUDY: THE DAN PLAN AND BECOMING AN EXPERT AS AN ADULT

BECOMING AN EXPERT AS AN ADULT

In June 2009, Dan McLaughlin was golfing with his brother in Omaha, Nebraska, when he made a life-changing choice. During that afternoon, Dan and his brother had entertained a question that was important in a lot of people's minds: Can someone become really good at something even when starting as an adult? If so, how good can they become? And what would be the best way to go about doing it? Dan would seek the answers to these questions through his own quest to become a golf pro.

Dan was a great candidate with whom to test Anders Ericsson's theories on the effect of practice on becoming an expert. Dan was a novice at golf and not a trained athlete. He certainly was no couch potato. He had played some tennis and had run cross country during his freshman year of high school. On the other hand, he also was not simply changing sports.

Dan planned to collect records from the very beginning. This would allow him to chart his progress from novice to expert. It would be the chance to establish whether the rules that apply to those who start in childhood also apply to an adult.

Dan's goal was to appear in the PGA Tour's qualifying school. To do this would mean reaching a handicap of 2.5, meaning he would have to be among the top 6 percent of players in the United States. In other words, 94 percent of the golfers would be rated worse than him.

Getting to that level of golf expertise would be no simple task. Thus, Dan spent time planning the best way to execute his plan. He knew that achieving his goal could not be done without help from the outside. Little did he know that he would end up working directly with Anders Ericsson, the researcher who was an expert on experts.

DAN'S PRACTICE PLAN

To get more input, Dan set up a website that laid out his philosophy and detailed his road to becoming a golf pro. As soon as he set up his website, advice began to come in. His plans eventually led him to the motor-skill expertise literature. He connected with Dr. Leonard Hill, who had worked on the nature of golf experts under the supervision of Anders Ericsson while at Florida State University.

To achieve his goal of appearing in the PGA Tour's qualifying school, Dan took Ericsson's work to heart. What stood out to him—like it stood out to most people—was the notion of 10,000 hours. This concept was popularized by Gladwell because of its simplicity, and Dan began to plan his route to this magical number. It was easy to target this number even though it was never part of Ericsson's claims.

Dan's initial plan was to practice six hours a day so that he could reach his goal of 10,000 hours within three and a half years. After speaking to Hill, Ericsson, and his own coach, Dan modified his plan. He learned quickly that Ericsson's theory was not so much focused on the quantity of practice. Rather, Ericsson's work had focused on the value of deliberate practice, which had very specific qualities.

Deliberate practice involves getting feedback on one's performance. Thus, not all hours of practice are created equal. Ericsson explicitly laments the fact that much of the time in practice is wasted. This can happen during long practice sessions that are too easy and lead people to simply tune out. It can also happen when practice is too hard and people fatigue. By requiring the learner to get feedback, deliberate practice helps to keep the learner on track. In Ericsson's view, deliberate practice is most effective when it involves a teacher, coach, or mentor.

Luckily, Ericsson was willing to serve as an adviser. Dan's actual coach could help with the specifics of golf practice. Armed with his plan, Dan could now start to work on the specifics of his plan.

To keep to his original plan of getting to 10,000 hours in three years, Dan decided that he would split his daily practice sessions into two. Morning sessions would last two to three hours with a break in the middle of the day. Afternoon sessions would last two hours. In between, Dan planned to rest but he would also add visits to the gym and some jogging.

Spreading out his practice accomplished two things. First, it helped to make sure that he could engage in deliberate practice. Spacing his practice also took advantage of one of the most powerful forms of learning, which is called *spaced*, or *distributed*, practice. It turns out that practicing for very long blocks of time is not as beneficial as practicing in separate segments of time. By splitting up his sessions, he allowed more time in between for a settling-down process that psychologists call *consolidation*.

Dan was using a lot of the science of learning to help guide his practice. It was a twenty-first-century test of an old question about expertise. The hope was that by using learning science, Dan might be able to reach his goal as an adult. With all the planning in place, he finally set out to begin his practice regime.

DAN'S ACTION PLAN

Dan's first practice sessions focused on putting. His coach emphasized that putting was very difficult to do. It required learning to hit the ball from distances that varied from thirty feet (about nine meters) up to a few inches or centimeters. The fact that there is so much variation in the distance makes putting very difficult.

Even the easiest putts can be difficult. While in principle it should be easy to hit a ball from extremely close, it is also the most nerve-racking part of the process. As we will see in a later chapter, it is very common for players to choke under pressure. When something is so easy that failing to achieve it would be terrible, the pressure increases even more.

To learn to putt, Dan began to systematically work backward. He started by putting from one foot away and reached 100 percent performance within a day. Only then did he move to three feet, and it ended up taking a few weeks to reach the 90 percent–plus range. He continually progressed to farther and farther points for four and a half months until he could hit the ball off the ground.

Dan spent the first year and a half practicing. It wasn't until he hit eighteen months that he played his first full course.

He also tracked his handicap while keeping track of his hours. Below I created a graph based on the data published on his website. I also plotted two lines to fit the data. One is a linear equation, which can be seen as a straight line. The other is a nonlinear equation that is a dotted line that curves.

Below and above the lines are two equations that are a best fit for the data. The fit is indicated by R^2, which tells us how much change in one variable is related to change in the other variable. In this case, the hours of practice capture about 75 percent of the effect of handicap for the linear function, which is $y = ax + b$. If we add in a polynomial function (the one with more variables as indicated, with x^4, x^3, etc.) which you can see below the lines of Dan's performance, we can increase this to 86 percent.

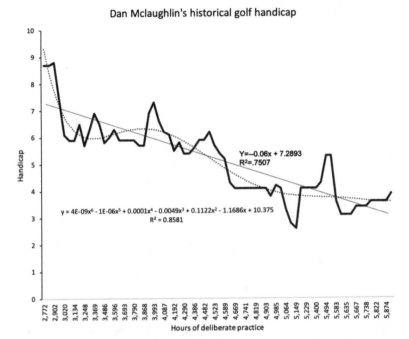

Dan McLaughlin's drop in handicap as his hours of deliberate practice increased during the period from April 2012 to May 2015. *Courtesy of the author.*

Despite both models capturing a lot of the data, notice how the actual data goes above and below this line. These jagged points show how Dan's handicap goes mysteriously up and down. For example, at 3,993 hours into his 10,000-hour experiment, his handicap goes up to 7.3 one day. However, on that very day, Dan reports feeling that he had played magnificently. Other regular practice days were marked by an improved handicap.

As we go forward there are other jagged peaks, and his lowest point comes in at around 5,200 hours with a handicap of 2.6 on June 1, 2014. Then, his handicap goes up from there and eventually comes down again. Even though the general trend is down, it takes time for this to happen.

In 2015, a little over halfway to his 10,000-hour goal, Dan suffered a back injury. He tried rehab, stretching, and physical therapy. Nothing seemed to help his sore back. He tried taking time off but was never able to heal fully. He bid farewell to his plan with a difficult post that began with the words, "Over the past two months I have started this post at least 10 times."

DID THE DAN PLAN FAIL?

On the one hand, Dan's plan can be seen as a failure. Dan abandoned his plan at just over six thousand hours when his back gave out. His goal was to reach 2.0 in order to achieve his objective. He never made it past 2.5. He never qualified for the PGA Tour's qualifying school.

On the other hand, everyone agreed that Dan made incredible progress and that he finished as a much better golfer than when he began. Robert Bjork, an expert in memory and learning and an avid golfer, was impressed by how much progress Dan had made. That a novice could get that good in so little time was noteworthy. However, for many people Dan had failed to show that there was no such thing as talent. He never became a pro via deliberate practice.

Lost in this entire discussion is the notion of development. If we take experts studied by Ericsson or any other study of exceptional performance, almost every one of those studies relies on individuals who showed exceptional achievement before adulthood. One possible explanation for the "failure" of the Dan plan is that he began much too late to ever become an expert.

However, there is another aspect of the Dan Plan that I have not really seen covered extensively. Very little discussion has focused on the speed with which he expected to execute his plan. The original plan was to reach 10,000 hours within three and a half years. Yet, most world experts do not reach the height of their abilities until after ten years or so.

There is an insight into how his training might have come a bit too late for Dan. In October 2015, he attended the 1st Scientific

Conference on Motor Skill Acquisition in Kisakallio, Finland. He titled the entry in his blog "Nonlinear Pedagogy," which is based on the idea that learning does not go in a straight line. The idea is that learning new skills involves doing different types of activities. It is the topic that David Epstein takes up in his book *Range*. The idea is that early specialization is not the rule but the exception.

Maybe Dan's failure was not that he started too late but that he rushed into a process that was meant to take several years. And during these years he would not just play golf but mix in many other activities, much like children do. Children are not just younger but they also learn differently from adults. Nonlinear pedagogy shares a lot with a very old idea termed *emergentism*.

Emergentism is focused on nonlinearity because it views change as involving a lot of little things coming together to form a greater whole. These combinations do not just add up to a result. They lead to a transformation, a fundamental change in the way that things are organized.

In Dan's case, it would have involved him playing other sports, doing other activities, and even taking extended breaks. It is a form of extremely spaced learning intermingled with other things. As we will see later, this approach was very helpful for Ash Barty, a professional tennis player. It will be a few more chapters before we get to Barty. First, we need to consider the notion of emergence and how that influences our view on building skills.

EMERGENCE IN HUMAN LIFE

EMERGENCE IN THE NATURAL WORLD

Things that mushroom suddenly are called *emergent phenomena* by scientists. We can think about our bodies as the combination of biological and chemical processes. For each of us, movements, thoughts, and sensations are the product of chemical and electrical activity. It is the combination of these elements across time that leads to our ability to learn new things.

The notion of how things recombine at the level of chemical elements was considered by John Stuart Mill, one of the premier philosophers of the nineteenth century. This is best represented in his work titled *A System of Logic*.

While studying in France during his adolescence, Stuart Mill had spent time hiking. On his hikes and in his studies, Stuart Mill encountered two different types of relationships. Some relationships occurred in succession. For example, he might be hiking and accidentally kick a rock that would hit another one. In this case, one could establish cause and effect. His foot hit a rock, which caused the rock to fly and hit a second rock. The movement of the second rock was subsequently caused by the movement of the first rock.

Two key concepts that come from Stuart Mill's classic work center on simultaneity or succession. In simultaneity, two things can appear at the same time. In the example above, the dirt flies up at the same time as the rock is kicked. In succession, one thing must come after the other. This happens when the kicking comes before the rock's flying. In Stuart Mill's view, succession and simultaneity are key for our understanding of science and the natural world.

In general, scientists try very hard to establish cause and effect. To do this they rely on succession, the idea that the cause comes first and the effect afterward. The establishment of cause and effect works best when we reduce a problem to its basic parts. For example, we can think of hours of practice as the cause and improvement in skill as the effect. Reducing something to its basic parts is called *reductionism*.

Emergentism stands in contrast to reductionism by looking at multiple causes for one effect. In these complex relationships, the actual causes are difficult to determine because the building blocks change dramatically during the transformative event. Stuart Mill's ideas show us that even at the level of chemical elements, things combine and recombine to form something new. Water emerges from the combination of oxygen and hydrogen when these two elements stop being gases and together form a liquid.

The link from the natural world to our human world was not the topic of Stuart Mill's system of logic. It was Pierre Teilhard de Chardin who pushed the idea of emergentism even further. In thinking about evolution and our place in the world, Teilhard de Chardin made the link between combinations at the chemical level up to our lives as humans and in our ability to learn new skills.

INFOLDING, HUMANS, AND EMERGENTISM

As a paleontologist, Pierre Teilhard de Chardin subscribed to the Darwinian point of view, which operated at the level of species.

There was only one problem. He was a priest at a time when evolution was seen as heresy. Although French society was very engaged in his ideas, the Catholic Church did not appreciate a priest advocating for the theory of evolution.

Rather than move him up the academic hierarchy to a professorship or some other higher erudite post, the Catholic Church put him on assignment in China. It was a way to silence him before he created more problems. However, this punishment was not enough to rob him of his views. Teilhard de Chardin did not give up on his faith. Rather, he discovered his connection to a larger world while exiled.

Banished to another continent, he continued his work both scientifically and spiritually. As he looked across the barren desert, he could see a wasteland with nothing of value. When he overturned a rock, he discovered nothing below it. And yet he knew that this world was teeming with life. Out of the landscape like the one in front of him, life had been born. He called this layer around the earth *pre-life*.

Teilhard de Chardin did not stop at the inorganic world. He imagined how the desolation of pre-life in which molecules combined and recombined had led to the emergence of life. The living planet full of plants and animals came to form the second wave that enveloped the globe. Thus, pre-life led to a second sphere around the world that he termed *life*. In his view, each of the phases of evolution came to form a series of spheres that surrounded our planet.

Finally, Teilhard de Chardin came up with a key insight that adds to our thinking. He describes each sphere as folding into itself. As the different building blocks of life began to combine, they essentially disappeared and were transformed. In short, it is as if each sphere was swallowed up by the previous one.

The process was one of continual change as the world folded into itself over and over again. Subatomic particles fold into atoms, atoms fold into themselves to form molecules, and so on and so forth. As we will see in a bit, this idea of infolding also applies to how we as humans develop. This development, in turn, has implications for the nature of skill building and how we learn new things. Rather than it being a process in which things are simply added up, learning a new skill involves a series of transformations. We will come back to that idea a bit later in the chapter and also later in the book.

INFOLDING AND THE DEVELOPING BRAIN

The basic systems that are used for every skill that we will learn as children and adults is set very early in life. Our brains become intricately wired across time. Building blocks at the cellular level transform our brains from sensing and movement into thinking. It is this sensing and movement that we later leverage to learn a new sport, a new musical instrument, or a new language.

At the dawn of our journey into the world, a sperm and egg join, thereby bringing together genetic material from each parent. All humans have two sets of chromosomes that are inherited via the sperm and egg. Contained in these chromosomes are genes that have strands of DNA, chains of amino acids that form the building block of the living universe. After the sperm and egg join, a series of biological and chemical processes take a single cell from an embryo to a fetus and then to a newborn in just the span of forty weeks or so.

Our DNA contains the genetic code that helps to guide our development. However, DNA influences development indirectly. Although DNA contains instructions for the sequences that build proteins, it cannot actually make those proteins. DNA is formed by two interlaced strands that unzip, leaving one side open to pair with free-floating RNA strands. These single strands are the ones that transport instructions to make a protein.

Thus, during early development the strands of DNA in cells create strands of messenger RNA that build the proteins that compose tissues inside of us. The DNA literally unzips itself and creates messenger RNA strands that build the tissues that come to form our bodies.

Shortly after conception, the cells that form our beings are undifferentiated. This undifferentiated tissue is composed of stem cells. Later, these tissues begin to specialize as the cells move to different locations.

The first stage of development involves the creation of a blastocyst, a single glob of cells. This glob of cells quickly divides into three layers. The innermost endoderm leads to the formation of the organs including the liver, heart, and lungs. The middle layer, the mesoderm, leads to the formation of the muscles and skeletal system. The outer layer, the ectoderm, leads to the formation of the nervous system.

As we think about brain development up until this point, we can witness how each stage folds in on itself. The first few cells divide, creating a single glob of cells that then changes into three layers. The three layers themselves begin to specialize. The view is not that dissimilar from the one that Teilhard de Chardin saw when staring at the desert. Where there was no life, life emerges. From two cells, a collection of cells with more and more complex layers continues during our fetal development. From this complexity emerges the nervous system, and out of this the brain.

OUR BRAINS, OVERLAPPING SPHERES

Infolding, the phenomenon during which combinations of simple elements disappear as they combine into more complex wholes, is one that also holds during brain development. The blastocyst, a grape-like structure, very quickly morphs into another arrangement. The outermost of three layers mentioned earlier, the ectoderm, begins the process of creating a nervous system. To do this the flat layer folds into a tube that later becomes the nervous system. Because of its physical form, biologists have come to term this the *neural tube.*

The groundwork for skill building can be seen in the way in which the tube comes to define our nervous system. This can be seen in two directions. The first is top to bottom. The top end of the neural tube turns into the brain and the sensing organs. The bottom end turns into the spinal cord. This axis remains for the rest of our lives as our head contains the brain and the spinal cord, and most of the rest of the nervous system is below that.

The second distinction, from front to back, lines up with our motor and sensory systems. In any skill that we develop, we must sense what is out in the world and then react to it. The importance of this sensorimotor distinction is great enough to lead to two distinct places along the neural tube. The top side, which is called the *dorsal side*, lying toward our backs, is mostly devoted to sensory processing. The bottom side, called the *ventral portion*, is dedicated to motor processing.

The top portion also shows additional infolding. In terms of brain development, layers formed very early lie at the core as later-developing layers wrap around this center. The way in which the later brain areas wrap around a core is reminiscent of our earlier discussion. The spherical process first proposed for evolution and the movement from pre-life to human culture is an interesting analogy here. In brain development, we see a similar process to that observed by Teilhard de Chardin.

One question that remains is how the brain is able to tune itself to learn new things. To understand the learning process more clearly, we need to zoom back into the level of the nerve cells. After this we will zoom back out to the brain again.

FROM SINGLE NOTES TO SYMPHONIES

We can think of our mental life as consisting of single notes embedded within a symphony. The human brain is composed of billions of nerve cells. They make up the building blocks of our mental life. The neuron as a piece of machinery is relatively simple. At the center is the cell body, which contains the nucleus. The nucleus is crucial in that it produces the proteins that allow neurons to function.

Each end of the neuron contains dendrites. These tentacle-like extensions are the ones that provide a connection to other neighboring neurons. The tentacles of the dendrites take in information via chemical signals emitted by other neurons. If these signals add up to a large-enough sum, they will generate an electrical impulse. These electrical impulses are shuttled down a long tubelike structure called an *axon*. These axons are enveloped by a fatty sheath that helps to keep the signal from seeping out. Once the electrical impulse reaches the end of the axon, it will stimulate the dendrites on the other end of the neuron, causing chemicals to be released. And then the cycle begins again when other neurons receive a chemical message.

We owe a lot of our knowledge of the structure of a neuron to Santiago Ramón y Cajal. A Spanish neuroscientist and winner of the Nobel Prize in Medicine, he almost did not become a doctor. His father, Santiago Ramón y Casus, had put himself through medical school at great personal sacrifice. Santiago Ramón y Cajal, his son, had no interest in medicine. To him medicine meant treating sick patients, a task that he did not find appealing. His major goal was to become an artist. He wanted to study art. His father and his teachers were up in arms over his choice of a career with such a bleak future. Ramón y Cajal was stuck between dying of hunger as an artist or tending to dying patients as a doctor.

Little did Santiago know that all his wishes could come true: be an artist, be a doctor, and not treat sick patients. After finishing medical school and obtaining a professorship, Ramón y Cajal was able to work on a topic that had nothing to do with patients: looking at pieces of tissue under a microscope. To do this, he used a method that was developed by Camilo Golgi to see cells in the nervous system.

Golgi, who was also a doctor, had worked with patients. However, in his spare time, he experimented with various staining methods in a hospital kitchen. He used metals and began to find that he could see structures in the nervous system. Other researchers had not been able to see these tissues. Golgi saw different regions of the brain as well as the axons and dendrites. Based on his findings he concluded that the brain was an interconnected web of nerve fibers.

Using Golgi's method, Ramón y Cajal decided that he needed to improve it. He made several adjustments. What he discovered would contradict Golgi's main assertion. Rather than finding an interconnected web of nerve fibers, he was able to find that there were single neurons.

During this period, Ramón y Cajal described a form of flow in which he would spend hours looking under the microscope. He also found a use for his artistic abilities. He felt great pleasure in drawing the neurons he saw under the microscope. His ability to visualize these forms in a way vindicated him. He was able to become an artist and a doctor while avoiding the care of sick patients entirely.

The work by these two Nobel Prize winners is interesting because it brings up a debate that has lasted some time. On the one hand, Ramón y Cajal's neuron doctrine leads us to think that each neuron is an independent machine. Golgi, on the other hand, suggested that the brain is one interconnected fiber of nerves. The reality is, of course, a bit of both. Neurons are single processing units, and they are interconnected into a web. While neurons can act independently, they are affected by other neurons around them. Today we can peer into the brain and see how the brain processes information in real time. What researchers see when they look at this activity are waves of electricity that go back and forth on the shore that lies between our skulls and the outside world.

THE NEURAL BASES OF SKILL BUILDING

Skill building, as I have alluded to, is the product of what happens within the biological systems that exist within us. The components of learning can already be seen in the basic building blocks. The brain wraps around itself. Later-developing brain areas are wired up around a core with the more elementary basic systems that are built up first. These simpler, earlier-developing systems already code things that will be relevant for us later in life. An unborn fetus actually moves spontaneously in order to wire up the systems that will be involved in movement later on. They can also detect changes in light and sound that occur outside from inside the womb.

This does not just resemble the way in which molecules combine and recombine to create life. It actually forms a core part of the nature of skill building. Every skill we build will inevitably have contact with both early- and late-developing neural systems. In later chapters, we will touch on examples of how very basic mental building blocks morph into more complex skills.

Up until this point, we have talked about how neurons interconnect with other neurons as an ingredient in learning. The only minor issue with this view is that changes in how neurons connect are relatively slow. This leaves one very clear question: How is it that learning can happen so quickly if the connections change so slowly? It turns out that there is another mechanism for learning and skill building that was hidden from researchers for years. This mechanism is called *glia*.

Glia play a crucial role in brain development. They are the biological scaffolds that help make sure that neurons move to a particular place very early in fetal brain development. In the mature brain, they help with nutrition and other metabolic processes. Glia also help in the development of myelin, the fatty sheath that helps electrical signals travel more quickly down the axons in neurons.

The interesting thing is that glia are pervasive in the cortex. Even though they were thought to simply play a supportive role, recent work suggests that this support can help to fine-tune how neurons talk to each other. It is this fine-tuning that plays a role when we learn something new.

BEYOND NEURONS

When we pick up a new task, we inevitably have to rewire the brain. However, the connections between neurons borne by the connections across synapses can often take months or even years to occur. This is where a certain type of glia comes into play.

Let me use a freeway analogy here to illustrate the point. Imagine that you are in a city. Let's take Los Angeles, for example.

In 2004, the interchange between the 405 and the 101 (top left of the figure) was deemed one of the worst in the United States. I know this from personal experience. When I was fourteen, my father, stepmother, and younger half brother Luciano moved to Los Angeles, and I with them. For the next thirty years, I would spend some time in Los Angeles either living there or driving

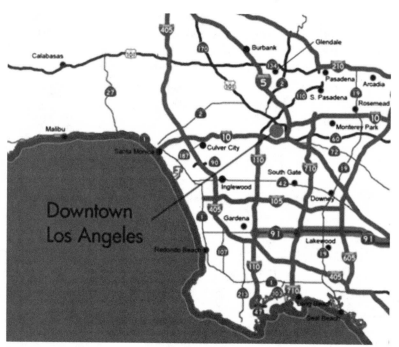

Map of the freeway system for Los Angeles, California. *Wikimedia Commons.*

through there from the south or the north. There was no time that the interchange between the 405 and the 101 was a smooth drive. One time we drove through at 2:00 a.m. on a Sunday and there was still some traffic. Never mind that during rush hour, the traffic in this area can slow to a crawl.

Now imagine that there was an accident at the 405–101 interchange, blocking traffic going into the city. If we looked at the map, we would see a big patch of cars packed in tightly right around the accident. Let's term this area the traffic hot spot. Word of this accident would quickly become known. Back in 2004, a driver heading into the city might hear this on the radio and plan accordingly. Thus, some of the traffic that was headed to this interchange would start to flow to other freeways.

To alleviate traffic, first responders could jump to the rescue. Paramedics, the fire department, police, and tow trucks could come in and clear up the accident. In the brain, this job would be done by microglia. Microglia are known for doing all types of repairs and cleaning up.

Once the accident is cleared and the traffic is flowing again, a city planner might ask what types of changes could help traffic in general. Of course, the logical answer would be to expand lanes or add a new freeway entirely. The planner might suggest creating more on-ramps and off-ramps to help cars find other ways to navigate around this area by connecting the freeway to other streets. These solutions would cost a lot of money (and time!).

Construction of actual roadways is slow and laborious. Ideally, there would be a way to alleviate this problem more quickly. It turns out that microglia also help in this regard. Imagine that instead of having to build anything, a large alien-like being came and just parked itself across this stretch of freeway. If such a being existed, then it could move to wherever it is needed.

It turns out that our brains have these alien-like beings floating around in them. "Alien-like" is how Pío del Río-Hortega first described glia. Río-Hortega, along with Nicolas Achúcarro, who were both students of Santiago Ramón y Cajal, were the first to discover microglia. Their work expanded on the ideas of neurons by introducing glia as essential elements that help to keep the brain nourished and free of waste products.

Today, newer research has found that glia can tune our neural connections. Because they act quickly, they can help certain neural connections to be dampened or increased depending on what is going on now. Glia thus are not just first responders. They can help strengthen the pathways that are needed at any given moment. Modern neuroscience sees that the brain is even more interconnected than we had previously thought. Thus, what happens when we concentrate too much on neurons is that we lose the emergent nature of our thoughts and blossoming skills.

Modern research has shown that the coding of movements, sensations, and thoughts in the brain involves multiple systems that wind and unwind themselves. Studying complex systems can be difficult, so there are times when scientists try to make their lives easier. To do this they take something complex and break it into its parts. Teilhard de Chardin, using a spherical model, would put it slightly differently. He would say that we are taking something round and making it flat.

UNFLATTENING EMERGENT PHENOMENA

The idea of infolding and spherical emergence is one that also applies to the way we think about skill building. Let's think about this using the most straightforward analogy, cartography. If we think about a map, it provides a flat view of the world, one that is appropriate if we are trying to drive to our favorite restaurant or walk to the local park. The previous section that considered a map of the L.A. freeway system was flat. At this smaller scale, a flat map does a pretty good job. So, we can use this flat-world approach for small problems like navigating from here to there by car or by foot.

City	Airport Code	Latitude	Longitude	Flight Time (hrs)	Distance (km)	Measured Distances String (cm)	Flat (cm)
Johannesburg	JNB	-26.134	28.242	--	--	--	--
Antananarivo	TNR	-18.797	47.479	3.2	2,156	6.5	3.2
Mahé	SEZ	-4.674	55.522	4.9	3,752	12.0	4.2
Dubai	DXB	25.253	55.364	8.1	6,389	20.5	4.9
Dakar	DKR	14.740	-17.490	8.5	6,705	21.5	5.6
Tel Aviv	TLV	32.011	34.887	9.1	6,473	20.5	4.4
Perth	PER	-31.940	115.967	9.2	8,326	26.0	12.4
Istanbul	IST	40.976	28.814	9.5	7,430	24.5	5.0
São Paulo	GRU	-23.382	-46.469	9.8	7,451	23.5	9.9
Madrid	MAD	40.494	-3.567	10.3	8,077	26.0	5.7
Singapore	SIN	1.359	103.989	10.4	8,661	27.5	9.7
Frankfurt	FRA	50.033	8.571	10.8	8,658	27.5	5.9
Zurich	ZRH	47.465	8.549	10.8	8,387	27.5	5.6
Amsterdam	AMS	52.309	4.764	11.1	8,986	29.0	6.1
London	LGW	51.148	-0.190	11.3	9,004	29.0	6.2
Sydney	SYD	-33.946	151.177	11.8	11,044	35.0	15.8
Hong Kong	HKG	22.309	113.915	12.8	10,672	34.5	9.8
Beijing	PEK	40.067	116.600	14.1	11,699	37.5	9.5
New York	JFK	40.640	-73.779	15.8	12,824	41.0	9.9
Atlanta	ATL	33.637	-84.428	16.4	13,581	44.0	10.6

Flight times and distances between Johannesburg, South Africa, and various cities in the world. *Adapted from the original created by Robert Carter, https://creation.com/a-direct-test-of-the-flat-earth-model-flight-times#FlightDataTable*

The situation changes entirely if we start to think about much longer distances. Let's try this approach on a plane. Below are the flight times between Johannesburg, South Africa, and various cities in the world.

You will notice that the straight-line distances between various cities do line up to some extent for most of the cities. For example, flights to Atlanta take 16 hours whereas flights to Dakar take 8.5 hours. So in these two cases, the distances are about right. We could argue that there is some discrepancy between flight miles and straight-line distances. But overall, the flight time is proportional to the straight-line distance. However, if we look at the next two cities below Dakar we can see that both Tel Aviv and Perth take slightly longer at 9.1 and 9.2 hours, respectively. Similarly, we can see that Sydney is farther than Atlanta but actually results in a flight that is almost 4.5 hours shorter. Measuring in a straight line works but it is limited. To get the whole picture we need to take a spherical model of the earth. Using this we realize that cities that would appear to be far apart on a flat earth are actually closer together when we round out the map to account for the curvature of the earth's surface. Teilhard de Chardin applied this whole-earth view to humans.

The idea of flattening can be applied to ways in which people think about cognition and its influence on skill building. Basically, we can extract a set of principles that are applied to the ways in which humans develop unique skills. For Ericsson, it involved deliberate practice and the creation of mental images—or representations, to use the more psychologically appropriate term. The problem with applying this flattening is that we miss part of the picture. Like using a straight line to calculate distances for an airplane, using a formula to figure out skill improvement will inevitably lead us to miss a number of things. The examples in this book that consider the notion of emergence are held up by the idea of infolding and sphericity. Hence, our skills are not unitary and do not move across a straight line. Rather, emergentism considers the result of processes that fold in on themselves over time doing this again and again.

INFOLDING AND SKILL BUILDING

Our brains start out by relating to the world via sensory and motor systems. It is very basic at first. This first glance that we take at the world folds into itself and becomes the building blocks for more complex ways of seeing. At birth we might track the basic features that make up a face. We go from just black-and-white images with little motion and no identity to slowly folding this into the next level, which is to see motion, color, and so on. This process keeps folding in on itself like a sphere that keeps taking what it is on the surface and then pulling it into the center, revealing another layer that is currently being used. As the spheres concentrate the lower levels of information, the higher levels of information begin to appear. We begin to combine sensation with movement and so on and so forth.

Our bodies have a similar process when it comes to motor skills. The nerve fibers needed to react to sensations to generate the correct action at first fire to very basic things. Then, over time our brains and bodies begin to integrate these processes. This can be observed in chess champions who *see* more than a novice does. The basic process of seeing forms, shapes, and patterns is increasingly folded into itself until what is revealed is the chessboard as if it were a set of patterns. To the chess player, a chessboard is like a face or a word to the rest of us: a pattern laid out with meaning that started somewhere and is going somewhere else.

In language, we take basic sounds and combine them into bigger and bigger chunks. These sounds are then linked to the written forms you are looking at right now. You can read them effortlessly. It becomes so automatic that breaking sentences apart becomes increasingly problematic. Trying to count how many *t*'s there are in this sentence becomes very difficult. In a written sentence, the letters get lost in the words and the words lost in sentences. Ideally, the paragraphs melt into pages and the pages into chapters, and before you know it the book is done.

The nature of infolding is also one that exists in the anatomy of our brains. While a single cell can by itself take in chemical signals on one side, produce an electrical impulse that goes down its body, and then send chemical signals out the other side, it does not do its work entirely alone. Nerve cells are embedded in large networks. Thus, single cells and their actions are also the product of transformation. As more and more neurons interact, the growing waves move along larger and larger paths. When we add glia to the equation, the system gets even more complex.

The idea of infolding also happens to play a role in developing a particular skill. I found it particularly useful when working on my tennis serve. The tennis serve appears on the surface to be an easy shot. As people dig deeper, they will come to realize that the serve is not one thing. It is a collection of different motor programs that are combined and recombined to create what some have deemed one of the most complex skills in all of sport.

4

CASE STUDY: THE TENNIS SERVE AS AN EMERGENT FUNCTION

HITTING A BIG HOLE WITH A VERY SMALL BALL

The tennis serve has a privileged place in the minds of players and fans alike. It is the one stroke that symbolizes the aggressive dominance of a game that prides itself on composure and control. If you watch professional tennis players serve, it seems so powerful and impressive. Particularly impressive is the sound a high-level serve makes. It is as if someone popped a champagne bottle. Sudden, vicious, and explosive. To achieve this feat, tennis players are allowed to hurl the ball in the air but must keep their feet outside the court before striking the ball to create a shot that goes over the net and lands inside the service box. To achieve height, players are allowed to jump (not step) into the court and hit the ball in the air before landing inside the court. Servers get two chances to get a serve in the box. If they miss their second serve, they lose a point.

The most amazing part of the serve is how little space players have to achieve their feat. Traditional tennis is played on a court that is 78 feet (10.97 meters) in length by 36 feet (23.77 meters) in width. However, 4.5 feet on the left and right end of the court is used only for doubles, and this effectively shrinks the court to a width of 27 feet (8.23 meters) for singles. The distance the serve can travel is even shorter because the service box is just 54 feet (16.46 meters) away. At a diagonal you can stretch that a bit more. Oh, and I almost forgot. You have to hit the ball over a net that is 42 inches (106.5 cm) high at the posts and 36 inches (91.5 cm) high in the middle of the court.

What most struck me about the serve when I first watched tennis at UC Berkeley in college was how Steve Devries, the number one player at the time, seemed to curl the ball into the service box. To hit the ball in a straight line and still make it in the service box is only within the grasp of tennis players who are close to seven feet tall. Luckily, the tennis serve does not travel on a straight path. I noticed this because whenever I heard the familiar pop, I expected the tennis ball to go high in the air like a baseball. Instead, it would dive down, not up. It was like a curveball, or the bend kick made famous by David Beckham that would start high and then literally fall off a table and land inside the service box on the other side of the court. Many years later, I would observe the same thing with tennis pros Novak Djokovic and Stan Wawrinka. Both would hit the ball very high above the net with a sudden dive into the box seemingly at the last minute.

The serve gives us a contradiction. The ball is very small, the hole we have to hit in is very big, and the net is somewhat low. On the surface, this shot is relatively easy. And it is. The problem is that there is another person on the other side of the net. That person wants to win a point and as a returner will pressure us to serve better and better. It is the battle between the server and returner that defines the beginning of every point in a tennis game. The fact that we have all the control up until we hit the serve and lose it entirely once the ball is gone just adds pressure. It's enough to make even the best servers hiccup and miss serves left and right.

To overcome this pressure, we could easily adopt an Ericssonian approach. We could engage in deliberate practice. We could also hire a coach to help us improve. While on the surface all these things would help, they do not always do so. In fact, in some ways, they can often lead us backward and make the serve even worse. As we'll see next, the way out of the pit of a mediocre serve is not straight. It is up and down with a lot of bumps along the way. The main problem is figuring out how to practice it.

FINDING THE RIGHT TYPE OF PRACTICE

Given the importance of the serve, you can often catch people on the courts by themselves practicing it over and over again. I was one of those players. After playing tennis for more than twenty years, I was frustrated with my serve. It felt like so much work it became my personal goal to improve my serve over a ten-year period. The problems were entirely my fault. By the time I was in my late twenties, I had been playing for a little over ten years. My serve worked well in singles, but in doubles it was not so good. My trips to Mexico were happening less often as my work duties grew heavier and my parental responsibilities increased. One day I asked a tennis pro to help me with my serve. We worked for an hour and then I never resumed lessons. As I continued to practice my "new serve," a lot of bad habits crept in. I could hit a serve with a lot of spin, but it had very little speed on it. This was punctuated by a friend of mine saying I had developed a hitch. Ten years later it had gotten to a breaking point. I was still less than satisfied with it. That is when I began my tennis serve rehabilitation program.

The first thing I did was to sign up for tennisplayer.net. This website run by John Yandell was a treasure for tennis coaches and players alike. During his early years, Yandell published a book called *Visual Tennis*, which has pictures of what all the different strokes should look like at different points in time. Something like a freeze frame of different shots before video was widely available. Yandell held that tennis was visual and kinesthetic and that using these modalities would help to improve players' games. You might think this is for beginners, but it turns out that his methods work for everyone. In 1991, his methods helped John McEnroe regain his serving prowess. If it could work for McEnroe, it might work for me.

When I look around at the courts in my neighborhood, serve practice is nothing like what Yandell does. Most people think of the racket as a frying pan that has to hit an egg in midair and crack it. This is a simple serve. Throw the ball out in front of you and hit the ball forward into the box. What is so hard about that? The serve will go in, but at advanced levels it will lead to a world of pain, as I learned in my own matches. My serve did not have a frying pan aspect to it. But it was very tight and effortful. I found serving exhausting.

As I looked at the serve (actually at all tennis strokes), I realized that it is the quintessential emergent function. While the simple serve is easy, the advanced serve like the one hit by Steve Devries or John McEnroe is not. What I learned along the way is how complicated the serve is. Brian Gordon, a tennis coach with a PhD in biomechanics, has studied the serve for many years. He states that the advanced serve is one of the most complex skilled movements in all of sport. Don't get me wrong—it is not *the* most complex skill, just *one* of the most complex skilled movements.

Tennis matches had revealed a chink in my serve. It was good but just not as good as I wanted it to be. Over the following years, I did all kinds of different drills. I changed coaches, even garnering advice at a distance. The best advice came from Tomaz Mencinger, a coach from Slovenia who uses his degree in engineering to reengineer adult players' games. Tomaz eventually became my friend, and as we talked about tennis I came to realize a key aspect of his training.

Tomaz wrote about breaking strokes up into different pieces and working on each of these pieces. He was always trying to understand how each player sees the strokes. Similar to Yandell, he tried to understand what players were seeing in their minds and how to change that image. To change a stroke involved practicing very small parts of it. As time went by, each of these new pieces would blend into the larger stroke. It was a form of physical chunking that would affect the image of a stroke. His ideas build on the notion of mental representation and deliberate practice that Anders Ericsson highlights in his work.

Eager to continue improving my serve, I sent him a video and asked him to give me his feedback. His response was simple and very unsatisfactory. He told me that my serve was too tight. I needed to loosen up. He sent me videos of Federer warming up and asked, "Why does he start so slow? Why would the player with the most weeks at number one in the world hit the ball with almost no pace to start?" He began to assign all kinds of counterintuitive exercises. One was to serve with absolutely the least amount of power. Hit it just hard enough so that it barely goes over the net. Another one was to get a huge rubber band and have someone hold me at my waist while I served. I found other exercises on the Internet on my own. In one drill, I would throw and then serve in succession. During this time, I developed what I called my "nothing" serve. I would literally do nothing and try to hit the ball as loosely as possible. There were times that I practiced my "nothing" serve with an opponent. At first, I thought my opponent would blast these serves back. Instead, I noticed that this "nothing" serve had "something" on it. This slow practice made me realize that something odd happened when I loosened up. I had played baseball and football, and the only strange thing is that I had never really thought about the effect of throwing on serving. What I found out surprised me.

FINDING THE CORE OF THE SERVE

The serve is a very complex stroke. It starts from a player's feet and then extends up into the tips of the player's fingers to create a tremor in the racket at the point of impact. The key ingredient is one that is almost invisible to the eye. For years, people had told me that the serve uses a throwing motion. That made no sense to me. Then one day I realized that I had never understood how to throw.

So how do you throw a ball? Grab a ball and throw it and describe it to me. The arm goes back and then it goes forward, and the ball comes out of your hand. Now after you let go of the ball, think about what happens to your hand. If you throw the way I used to throw, your hand would finish down. But look closely at any pitcher or quarterback. Below is the picture of a football being thrown.

Throwing of a football. *Wikimedia Commons.*

Notice how after the player throws the football, his wrist twists outward. You might think this has to do with throwing a spiral with a ball that is not round. But if you look at a pitcher you will see the same thing.

Now look at the tennis serve.

Notice how the wrist flips out away from the body. This is called *pronation*, but it actually starts with the shoulder and arm and results in this very odd finish. If you place the palm of your right hand on your head and then slowly rotate your hand and arm to the right side (to the left if you are a left-hander), you will feel what

Throwing of a baseball by a pitcher. *Wikimedia Commons.*

Hitting of a serve. *Getty images.*

this rotation is like. The odd part is that the rotation of the hand to the side does not seem to make sense since the ball is going forward. Thus, throwing a ball is not just throwing it forward. There is a side component that creates an extra dose of acceleration across the entire arm.

Over the years, I have incorporated this component into my play and tested how it affects the way I throw. More than anything it feels like I can throw farther and higher doing this than if I just throw the ball with a forward motion. If this is new to you, you could try it out. It might serve you well for throwing things. I use it to throw larger pieces of organic waste to the end of my backyard. Using my new throwing motion I can hurl the not-so-good fruit that sometimes goes bad in the hot Houston summer. I can reach the trees in the back of my yard easily with minimal effort.

The important part of this motion is that it occurs very quickly and the arm acts like a lever. To achieve this the arm must be very loose, and it has to travel along a longer path. The longer the lever, the greater the acceleration, and the farther the throw. Basically, the high-level throw and the tennis serve are trying to maximize the distance that the arm travels to create the maximum velocity.

One question you might ask yourself is how the loose and slow motion led to a better serve. For a long time, I asked myself the same question. Why is it that serving slow and fluidly had made my serve faster and more powerful? The answer lies in the way in which our nervous system works.

SLOWLY REWIRING A MOTOR-SKILL

The pop-of-the-cork sound is due to the vicious and rapid turn of the racket outward. The turn has to be timed within a very narrow window so that the ball hits the strings. If the racket does not turn just right, it can lead to a serious mishit. In one case, Sam Stosur, a professional women's tennis player known for her massive spin serve, hit the frame of her racket, sending the ball high in the air. This shank went over her opponent and the line judges and landed in the stands. This example illustrates how the acceleration is so massive and fast that a mistake causes us to mistime the serve drastically.

I had hit an intermediate serve from the beginning. This initial serve had basically been taken from my existing motor programs of throwing and jumping. As a kid I had played basketball and football recreationally. I had also spent a lot of time throwing rocks, climbing hills, and riding skateboards as well as bikes. When I first started to serve, it seemed natural to combine all the different skills to hit a pretty simple serve.

As players scale the long tennis ladder, matches become more competitive and the need for a spin serve becomes more important. This is especially true in doubles, where the spin serve gives us time to get to the net, and it is a key difference from singles, where players tend to play farther back.

Adding a spin serve altered these existing programs. I was trying to add spin to the ball, but in doing so I was very stiff and tight. The original lesson I took in my late twenties had essentially given me a quick fix. I then went on to repeat that motor program over and over again.

When we learn new motor skills, our brain creates two different circuits. One involves actual synaptic connections. The neurons are woven together in such a way that the combination of muscle movements can be executed. The second mechanism is astrocytes, the glia that help to take care of nerve cells. It turns out that astrocytes also help to form new synaptic connections.

This might help to explain why slow practice is so valuable, especially when learning a new skill or trying to change an existing skill. In both cases, our brain needs to rewire itself to accommodate the new neural firing pattern. When we practice at full speed, we are acting as if the skill is already perfected. However, a new skill is still in the wiring phase. During these early phases, it is still not efficient enough to be repeatedly used. Here is where very slow fluid practice can help. It allows the circuit to be formed without the need for it to be done quickly.

As time goes on, we can slowly ramp up the speed. It is worth noting that slow practice is done even at the pro level. Monica Seles, a phenom who won several major tournaments before she was stabbed on the court during a tennis match, purportedly would spend half her practice with very slow balls hit on half the court. Ben Hogan, a champion golfer, would practice with a very slow swing that was almost identical to his regular golf swing. My son Nikolas would practice so loosely that he would hold his racket with his thumb and one other finger. He would also often serve very slowly even during matches.

Combining such fine movements into a single whole requires time. For children, the time is forced on them. They simply cannot play an adult game until they are, well, adults. Adults, however, are often in a rush to establish that circuit and then move on to other things.

Synapses and their wiring take time. It is especially time consuming with a skill like a tennis serve. The wave of electro-chemical signals in the brain has to be mapped to a set of coordinated body parts. These parts generate a wave from the feet, up through the torso, into the arm that accelerates, and then finally through the hand. From the hand, the wave flows through the racket grip, up the throat of the racket, and then to the racket face—an extension of the palms of our hand. This requires our muscles and nerves to receive these signals from the brain and then execute them.

A tennis serve then requires not just a physical adjustment but also a mental one. It is our brains and bodies working to coordinate themselves. Today after many years, I have finally learned to coordinate these complex movements into a whole. But even with my serve much improved there is constant change. I will take a lesson and learn one more little thing that adds to it. My serve is constantly organizing and reorganizing itself. The process is much more subtle today than it was ten years ago, but it is not static.

While we might think of these physical skills as separate from our mental skills, many of the same rules apply. Many of the higher-level skills that we will see later in the book will show the basic pattern of constant reorganization. The changes seen in childhood can be more dramatic compared to those seen in adulthood. However, these early changes set the stage for later learning. We will now turn to the pattern of learning seen in childhood.

5

CHILDHOOD, ADOLESCENCE, AND THE IMPORTANCE OF STARTING SMALL

THE LAW OF REGRESSION

Théodule-Armand Ribot was one of the first French psychologists to became intrigued by the way in which memory was lost in patients who suffered from amnesia due to epileptic episodes. In his book published in 1882, he wrote about how memory loss affected cognitive memories more than routine procedures. Patients could remember how to tie their shoes and how to get to the local pharmacy. However, they had a lot more trouble remembering events. Their amnesia was particularly acute right around the time of onset. One patient who suffered from a concussion was unable to remember what happened right before or after his fall and the blow to his head.

Ribot's view on memory loss is called the *law of regression*. The pattern could be best seen in the way language in patients broke down. The order was almost always the same: proper names, common nouns, adjectives and verbs, interjections, and, finally, gestures. For proper names, patients would forget the most recently learned ones first and the ones learned earliest in childhood last. The same pattern appeared for common nouns where early learned words such as "elephant" were lost much later than words like "abacus."

Seeing the phenomenon once is great from a scientific point of view. However, Ribot wanted to see if this law also appeared in other types of patients. Did the law of regression hold up for memory in general?

To test many of his views, Ribot turned to work with bilinguals who learned a first language and a second language at different points in time. He proposed that early and late learned languages differed in how well they would stand up to some type of brain injury. First languages that were learned in childhood would be most resistant to brain damage. Second languages, especially those learned in adulthood, would be least resistant.

Ribot came of age as a scientist before Piaget did his seminal work on child development starting in the late 1920s. Thus, there was very little work with children to verify Ribot's law of regression. Out of necessity, he turned to an existing literature on second-language acquisition, which at the time built on the distinction between speech (motoric memory) and understanding, which was a component of the mind. In fact, Ribot was hinting at the distinction between speech and other forms of memory. However, Ribot found his biggest confirmation in the way that speakers of multiple languages showed recovery. Of particular interest to him were patients who under anesthesia showed amazing recovery of a language even after protracted periods of little use. One example that he uses is a case he had read about.

An old forester had lived in his boyhood on the frontier of Poland, where he had never spoken anything but the Polish tongue. Afterward he lived in the German districts, and his children asserted that for thirty or forty years he neither heard nor pronounced a single Polish word. An incident sparked by anesthesia that lasted nearly two hours resulted in him speaking, praying, and singing entirely in Polish.

LEARNING EARLY MATTERS

Because of my experience with language learning at different ages, I had always been interested in understanding the effect that age has on second- and third-language learning. Researchers refer to the difference in learning something at different ages as an *age of acquisition effect*, or *AoA* for short. The basic idea is that what you learn early is different from what you learn later in life.

The effects of early learning also appear in a study that I conducted with Christian Fiebach in Leipzig in 2002. In this study, we asked a group of native German speakers to look at a set of visually presented letters that could either be a word (light) or a nonword (nable, wight, etc.). Their job was simply to look at each one and decide if it was a word or not. Participants were shown the words on a computer screen as their brains were being scanned using functional magnetic resonance imaging (fMRI), a technique that measures brain activity by looking at how much oxygen is in the blood that is feeding a particular brain area.

When Christian showed me the data, my jaw dropped. The early learned words showed greater brain activity in areas of the brain devoted to the processing of spoken language and in linking sounds to vision. The later learned words showed increased activity in frontal areas of the brain that are used when people try to read for meaning.

In other words, it is almost as if making a word decision relies more on sounding it out if the word was learned when a person was young. For words learned later in childhood, most likely in school, the brains of native German speakers suggest that they were trying to figure out what it meant. If the word had a meaning, then it must be a word. This study showed me that there were two routes to reading words. Words learned early in life used sight and sound to a greater extent. Late learned words were more dictionary-like. Based on these findings, Ping Li and I proposed a sensorimotor hypothesis to account for language learning.

PIAGET AND THE SENSORIMOTOR HYPOTHESIS

The sensorimotor hypothesis—that early learning is more reliant on how we sense and how we move—was based on a theory proposed by Jean Piaget. Piaget suggested that cognitive development is a process of adaptation. Trained as a zoologist, he took many of the ideas from biology and brought them into thinking about child development. One clear bridge between biology and human development was in his use of the terms *adaptation* and *accommodation* to describe how children learn. The use of these terms could be applied to species that are trying to adapt and accommodate to a new habitat. For Piaget, the process of learning had an interesting parallel with theories of evolution.

Piaget also divided development into a series of stages. The first is the sensorimotor stage in which learning for a child involves learning by linking the sights, sounds, smells, and touch of things with our own movement. This stage lasts until early childhood, when children move into a preoperational stage. During this next stage, children take the world at face value. Look at the illustration below and tell me which one contains more circles.

An example of stimuli shown to children in order to test size constancy. *Courtesy of the author.*

If you are like most adults, you will choose the one on the left. However, children who are in the preoperational stage, between the ages of two and seven, will often choose the set of items on the right. They confuse size for quantity and thus do not consistently use the strategy of counting each item.

Piaget observed that after the age of seven, children would choose the set on the left as having a greater number of items. He termed this the *concrete operation stage*, in which children could think about physical things without taking them at face value.

Researchers devised all kinds of different tests of conservation in which children were tricked into thinking that things changed. One experiment along these lines would involve a set of researchers putting a dog mask on a cat. Children were then asked if the dog-looking cat was a dog or a cat. Children after age seven would report that it was a cat. Those younger than seven would report that it was a dog. In other words, children in the preoperational stage are fooled by how things look. Those in the concrete operations stage are not.

The final stage of development is what Piaget called *formal operations*. In this stage, children can hold abstract thoughts. You can think about all the things that children begin to do after the age of twelve. They learn abstract math and can think strategically on the sports field. They can also ponder hypotheticals such as, "What would happen if aliens invaded our planet intent on conquering it only to find out that they were afraid of birds and needed humans to manage these pests for them?" Maybe my son with his pigeon-chasing skills could have risen to the top of a much-needed new profession. All these hypotheticals are things that children can begin to do, according to Piaget, after they turn twelve.

Although Piaget used zoology as a way to frame his ideas, his work looked at how children behaved in different situations. Work with the development of the brain in children fits in with his views. For example, a recent study by Long and colleagues found that the area of the brain involved in processing the sounds used in language, called the *superior temporal gyrus*, changes in the way it is connected to other brain areas. Early in life it shows very strong local connections, meaning that it is only strongly linked to areas around it devoted to sound. However, during childhood this area forms stronger neural bonds with other areas in the brain. Sounds become tied to other things such as objects in the world, people we love, and even the sound of sports we play.

The movement from local to widespread connections in the brain fits in nicely with the findings that Christian Fiebach and I had observed. Specifically, words that are learned early in life show increased activity in brain areas in the superior temporal gyrus, an area involved in listening and comprehending spoken language.

Long and colleagues also found that later in childhood there are changes in the way that two different areas of the brain, the frontal and parietal lobes, are connected. These two areas are known as *association areas* that help to link sensory and motor codes together in more complex ways. This area is involved in what we call *working memory*, or our ability to coordinate multiple things in our minds.

Working memory could also be thought to be related to children's ability to know that a cat is not a dog when it is wearing a dog mask. This would require maintaining in mind that a cat was right there and that a mask was put on the cat to make it look like a dog, and then imagining that if the mask were taken off it would be a cat again. In short, the cat is a cat that looks like a dog. This type of more complex thinking arises as a child's brain begins to form these long-distance connections.

GETTING OLDER MEANS WIDER CONNECTION

Houston, like many modern cities in the United States, is webbed together by an increasingly larger and growing freeway system. In a previous chapter, I described how brain activity is highly interconnected in a way that resembles how traffic flows in a city like Los Angeles. The analogy of traffic flow also works when we think about the way that a child's brain starts out and eventually becomes an adult brain. For example, when we first moved to the Houston area, we bought a home in a suburb in an adjacent county that is fourteen miles (twenty-three kilometers) from the University of Houston. At first the small city we live in operated like a small island that was separate from the rest of the city. There was traffic on the freeways but only during rush hour. The local traffic was limited to very specific times of day.

Over time our suburb grew, and it became more intercon-nected with the entire city. The freeways and roads were expanded greatly. And the traffic grew to be unsustainable. A commute that used to take me twenty-five minutes when we first moved here even during rush hour mushroomed to forty minutes.

In 2019, the city announced a new toll road that would be opened to improve traffic flow. The new toll road promised to reduce the traffic problem. The promise of improved traffic might be one of the greatest illusions of our everyday lives. Work by Duranton and Turner looked at the effects of road expansion on traffic. To do this, they used historical data to calculate the effects of increasing and decreasing transportation flow on human traffic. They looked historically at vehicle kilometers traveled in metro-politan statistical areas. In other words, they looked at how much a person like me would drive in the city of Houston.

By looking at the data historically, they could establish cause and effect. In other words, what is the effect of building a new toll road on traffic? Their answer led to a resounding conclusion. The "fundamental law of road congestion" reveals that increasing the number of lanes on which a car can travel has no effect on traffic. Duranton and Turner note that people like to move around, and having roadways gives them a way to do so. In the case of my small suburb, construction on shopping centers has started to the south of us in the next suburb. Even farther south I can see the first housing developments, which like ours a few years ago promise to be far enough from the city to enjoy a quieter life but close enough to be in the middle of it all in thirty minutes. Over time our once-isolated suburb is being absorbed by the larger metropolis. With all these new roadways people will simply move around.

So, let's take it one step further. Imagine a place where there is no human traffic. For example, think about how many people are traveling between here and the moon. In 2020, that would be no one. Now imagine that a shuttle traveled to the moon once a month. We would get an increase in traffic. If transportation increased (and were affordable enough!), would the traffic decrease? For sci-fi nuts like me, it would be a gold mine. Would I pass on a weekend trip to the moon with my kids if I could afford it? Of course not, and the new lunar city would become crowded quickly, and before we knew it there would be a traffic jam on our way to the moon. The fundamental law of road congestion is just a natural outcome of human systems. Systems made by humans are like all natural systems and like the brain. They are flexible. Which brings us back to the brain.

What happens when we take our moon traffic analogy and apply it to the brain? Create a road that is untraveled and fill it up with traffic. In a sense, this is what the brain does for all of us. We have roads of bundled neurons that result in what neuroscientists call *white matter tracts*. These bundles of neurons, like roads traveling between the different hubs of our own cerebral metropolis, look white in a brain scan. As we noted earlier, each neuron in our brains has a fatty sheath that helps to insulate the electrical impulses. These impulses travel across axons before hitting the synapses, which release chemicals that cross from one neuron to the other. Myelin is like a fatty glove that coats the axons, and when you put a lot of these axons together like a set of cables that are wound together, they appear like roadways.

Early in childhood, activity in a particular brain area stays local, much like the traffic in a suburb does when it is not strongly interconnected with a city. As children grow older, brain areas become interconnected with other areas that are far away. The brain becomes more like a cobweb of interconnected freeways and roads that operate together. And like my suburb or the traffic in Los Angeles, which is even worse, everything becomes part of an interconnected network. The flow of traffic becomes like a natural system. The key here is that this development involves the interconnection of areas that at first are devoted to sensory information and motor responses.

Over time the brain becomes more interconnected, and in doing that it handles information in more complex ways.

This development of the brain parallels what Piaget saw in behavior. Early in life children are driven by what an item looks like. A dog with a cat mask is a cat. However, over time, children begin to understand that an animal can look like a cat but be a dog. This involves being able to keep one idea in mind (a dog) while seeing a different image through our eyes (a cat). To do this involves brain areas that help negotiate between what is in the world and what is in our mind. Thus, memories formed later in life have additional layers of information that are not contained in early learned memories. As our brains grow complex with age, what gets stored has more complicated information. This idea brings us to language and how early and late learning differs.

EARLY VERSUS LATE LEARNED LANGUAGES

Reading stories from over one hundred years ago about the recovery and loss of languages was what initially got me interested in bilingualism and the brain. Earlier we talked about a Polish forester who had moved to Germany for many years. One day under anesthesia he began to use Polish, his first language, for two hours. All of this happened after thirty years of not being exposed to Polish.

A similar incident happened to me. In my case, there was no anesthesia, and my "episode" lasted for just a few seconds. It wasn't my native language that was recovered. Rather, it was Portuguese, a language that I was exposed to unexpectedly as a child through music.

Roberto Carlos, a singer from Brazil, had adapted his songs to Spanish. He was one of my uncle Luis Enrique's favorite singers. Luis Enrique would spend so many hours singing that I eventually came around. I learned a lot of Roberto Carlos's songs and began to sing them. When I went back to Northern California for the school year, my dad bought me Carlos's record in Spanish and I continued singing alone.

On a second trip to the local record store, I could not find any of Carlos's albums in Spanish. As I flipped through the set of records, I saw the same record I already had in Portuguese. Before I grew too disappointed, my dad grabbed it. Over the next few weeks, I proceeded to try and sing the Portuguese versions of the songs that I liked so much. My Portuguese singing episode lasted for a few months.

A little over ten years later, I was back learning Portuguese, this time in a college class. I had stopped singing in Portuguese but still dreamed of visiting Brazil. I applied to the junior year abroad program and was accepted. I would spend two years altogether living in São Paulo, Brazil. Over that time, I lost my Spanish accent and began to sound like a Paulista, the name people use when referring to those who live in São Paulo.

Many years later, after I came back from Brazil, I began to sing to my son at night before he went to sleep. It seemed to soothe him more than a bedtime story. One day I found the words to a Brazilian lullaby that I had heard on Roberto Carlos's record as a child. As I sang the song, I grew startled when one of the words came out with a very strange-sounding accent.

Roberto Carlos grew up in the northeastern part of the country. The regional accent is very different from the Paulista that I had grown accustomed to. The night I sang to my son, I began to sing the first few words of the lullaby, "E tão tarde amanha já vem." But *tarde* came out with a hard *r*. The *r* was more like the *h* in *have* in English. I sounded like Roberto Carlos!

In singing a childhood song in Brazilian Portuguese, I had gone through my own regression. In singing that lullaby to my son, I went back to my earliest memories of Roberto Carlos and my attempts to sing in his native language. The motor programs that had been wired up early in life woke up. And they influenced my pronunciation of a language that I learned as an adult. It was as if some little piece of the creation of my Portuguese was still there. These early primordial pieces served as the building block of a much larger set of skills that I developed later.

It turns out that these primordial pieces also appear in sport. Around the same time that I was working on the effects of early learning in language, Tom Byer was busy working on his own version of Ribot's law of regression. In Byer's case it had to do with soccer.

6

CASE STUDY: TOM BYER AND THE ART OF SMALL BALL

FROM PLAYER TO COACH

If someone had picked a place to find the next great soccer skills coach, they probably would not have picked Ulster County which lies about 100 miles north of New York City. This region that has around 180,000 inhabitants today is not a place that one would have chosen to groom a player back in the 1970s. That era was a time dominated by mainstream American sports. The football played was one in which you threw more than you kicked. Basketball and baseball were more popular. There were, of course, the winter sports such as ice hockey, skiing, and ice skating. In the United States, almost no one back then used the term *futbol* either.

Ulster County is where Tom Byer first took up his interest in soccer. Despite the sport's lack of popularity, Roundhout Valley High School had a soccer team on which he played during his adolescence. In high school, he led his team to two league championships. Tom did not want to stop playing, and he was able to continue first at the State University of New York's campus in Ulster and then eventually at the University of South Florida.

After graduation in his early twenties, Tom's passion for soccer led him to seek out playing professionally. He tried his hand at European soccer at the Leighton Football Club in the Spartan South Midlands League in the UK. Eventually, he moved to Japan, where he played for what was then the Hitachi Football Club.

With his soccer career in full sunset, Byer continued to feel a passion for the game. After retiring at the age of twenty-nine, he began to seek other roles that could keep him connected to the game. Byer began to develop a keen eye for coaching—not as a head coach but as what he describes as a technical coach. Little did Byer know he was becoming a de facto applied developmental psychologist in training using soccer as his testing ground.

The common thinking at the time was that soccer coaching was best done later in childhood and in adolescence. Byer had another idea. When he studied the great players, he realized that all of them started at a much younger age. For them soccer started in the home. This led Byer to conclude that coaching could start at much younger ages. As we will see in a later section, he discovered how to teach basic soccer training before age two. The quote below summarizes much of his thinking.

> Many top players have terrific skills—physical fitness, the ability to read the game, heading ability, etc.—but lack basic techniques. Why? Because they were never taught them! You tend to get one shot when you're young to learn these core skills. Many coaches and federations still believe that you can only teach these skills at a later age—9 or 10 or even later—but when they are older, kids are usually already playing games and learning other stuff. The core techniques have to come first.

What Byer had noted was the following order. Children would be enrolled in a soccer league sometime around age five or six. They would have a few practices. Then the games would start and the coaching would occur in the context of competition. What Byer observed, however, puzzled him. How could coaches put players in to play when many of these children between the ages of six and ten did not have the basic skills to succeed?

Byer also had issues with what children were practicing. In his opinion, coaches were too focused on teaching children to kick the ball. To Byer, kicking was secondary. He found the idea of practicing kicking the ball into the goal even less logical. Most of the time on a soccer field is spent trying to either get to the goal or to stop the other team from getting close to the goal. In his view, it was the art of moving with the ball that really mattered. What also mattered was to do it in a way that was appropriate for younger children.

In a way, Byer's idea lines up with earlier ideas discussed on starting from the core. For the serve, the core might be something like a throwing motion. For language, it might be something like the speech sounds. For golf it would be putting from a very close distance. It is the earliest and fundamental part to develop before going on to more advanced complex actions, like hitting different serves, producing sentences with grammar, and playing a few holes in golf.

Learning skills and then using them to play soccer was a process. It took time. And rushing it could end up frustrating children. As we will see next, rushing the process could also lead to even worse outcomes: physical injuries so debilitating that they might affect players the rest of their lives.

CHILD SPORTS

The pressure to become a superstar early is locked into our collective consciousness. Take the story of Tiger Woods, who is purported to have started to play golf at age two. Coached by his father like many prodigies, Woods went on to become a legend in golf. Andre Agassi's father Mike has been rumored to have put a tennis ball in his son's crib. The idea was that to become a champion, an athlete has to start early and practice a lot. Although there is no direct connection to Gladwell and his book *Outliers*, the 10,000-hour idea has been front and center. Anders Ericsson's approach that inspired

Dan McLaughlin to reach 10,000 hours might also have played a role in starting younger to become an expert at the earliest age possible.

In the new path, children start competing early. Many travel on club teams with yearlong grueling schedules. To compete well in these leagues, many clubs emphasize playing competitively from a young age. This includes practice several times a week and weekend tournaments. Many parents are choosing to place their children in a single sport at earlier and earlier ages.

Unfortunately, the increased practice comes with an increased cost. Like Dan McLaughlin's back, children's bodies are giving up on them. Under the stress of a workload generally reserved for an older body, children are getting injuries that were never seen before.

The cost of all this specialization began to show up in young athletes who were now opting to go under the surgical knife at younger and younger ages. Dr. Mininder Kocher from Boston Children's Hospital began to see a disturbing trend in his operating room. He noticed that there was an increase in surgeries to reconstruct the anterior cruciate ligament (ACL) of the knee. This increase was not in adult athletes. It was in younger and younger children who were undergoing these surgeries.

The ACL injury is very common in adolescent and adult athletes, especially in sports that have contact or require players to change directions quickly. Despite the constant trend in pro and semipro athletes, Kocher noticed that it was becoming all too common to have children come in for this very delicate reconstruction. This type of reconstruction was particularly tricky given that children were still growing and the joint would change with age as they grew. To validate his observations, he and two other researchers, Frances Tepolt and Lanna Feldman, collected data from a large number of pediatric surgeons. What they found stunned them. The number of pediatric cases had increased fivefold from around 500 to 2,500 between 2004 and 2014.

As I noted earlier, overtraining may also have contributed to Dan's back problem. His practice sessions lasted several hours a day. His dream was to become an expert golfer by reaching 10,000 hours in three and a half years. However, his progress might have been too fast. Visits to the chiropractor helped temporarily. But his back injury continued to flare up and over time his goal of reaching 10,000 or so hours escaped his reach.

The fact that Dan suffered from the same fate that youth athletes do is a paradox. Starting early does carry advantages. In general, motor skills picked up early in life can be retained for a long time. For example, it is not uncommon for a parent to initially outperform their young children when performing some new motor skill, like shooting basketballs, kicking soccer balls, or learning to say new words in a foreign language. However, over time, children will eventually surpass their parents.

The key here is the word *eventually*. The problem is in a mechanistic view of skill, one in which there is a rush to get to the magical 10,000 hours of practice. In this view, a child athlete needs to be a well-oiled machine that can do all the things that adults can do. In working with children, parents, teachers, and coaches have learned that progress can be slow initially.

When given enough time, children can eventually surpass adult learners. This clearly shows that children are not little adults in terms of learning something new. This growth approach to learning fits in with my view that skills are like organic beings that arise from combinations of lots of different elements. The notion of emergent functions is also one that fits in nicely with Piaget's work, which saw complex cognition emerge out of the combination of basic sensorimotor building blocks.

BYER TAKES HIS PROGRAM PUBLIC

The idea that a child was like a machine did not fit in with Tom Byer's views. Byer had observed coaches having children kick for hours. It's the type of instruction that could easily lead to an injury. In Byer's view, this type of repetitive practice was not always ideal.

When he observed the very best players, he saw more than just players who were good at kicking. Players like Pelé, Diego Maradona, Lionel Messi, and Marta Vieira da Silva did not excel in kicking. Rather, they were excellent at moving with the ball.

All players had to learn to kick the ball. But kicking is only secondary in soccer. To Byer the most important skill was to learn to manipulate the ball. That is, he emphasized the importance of learning to manipulate the ball first. Or as Byer says, quoting Neymar, one of Brazil's great players, Brazilians don't fall in love with football; they fall in love with the ball.

The question that naturally arises is, how early? Should children be taught to manipulate the ball at age five? Age three? Age two? The insight into how to teach the most basic skill in soccer to children would come to Byer by chance. One day he was signing small replica balls at an event sponsored by Adidas. It dawned on him that he could use these same balls with children. Children's feet were small. Rather than waiting until children could handle a big ball, Byer thought it would be better to have children start younger with a ball that was their own size.

To test his hypothesis, he tried it out on his own kids. He and his wife began to place these small balls in different parts of the house. Byer would then encourage his young children to walk around the house with the balls. The interesting part is that a lot of what the children did was not scripted. He gave them the space to play with the ball on their own.

As they grew older he would teach them more advanced things. His son Kaito was sixteen months old at the time. Byer taught him to roll the ball and pull it back. To Byer this was almost instinctual. Children will learn to pull something toward them when they feel there is a threat that it will be taken away. For example, when someone reaches for a toy, a child will pull the toy away and protect it. To Byer this was a key aspect of soccer. Rather than learning to kick the ball away when challenged, children had to learn how to protect the ball first.

Based on his work using the approach of an applied developmental psychologist, Byer began to develop a set of progressions for soccer. These progressions did not correspond to particular ages. However, his work showed that children can learn the basics of ball manipulation as young as sixteen months. By teaching them to walk with the ball, Byer felt that the ball would become an extension of their feet. In short, the ball skills needed to excel in soccer were sensorimotor in nature.

Byer's approach is similar to the approach I took with my serve. Throwing was the core of the motion, and the outward turn of my palm was the part I had missed. Later in teaching my own kids I focused intensively on getting them to be loose and to make sure they could learn this motion. Richard Williams had Serena and Venus throw American footballs. The movement needed to generate a spiral is very similar to the motion in a tennis serve. After this is developed we could add throwing balls overhead and maybe even use heavier balls to get people to generate force with their legs.

In my case, I had rushed into competitive play as an adolescent. Some of these core principles had been developed through other sports. However, there were specifics that involved having to take a step back. In one lesson during my tennis renaissance in my forties, Liz Burris, a local tennis coach, was trying to get me to do something. I then asked her to just drop feed balls—literally just toss them right in front of me so that I could do what she was asking. "So, treat you like a beginner?" she asked. "Yes," I responded.

It worked. I could feel exactly what she wanted me to do by focusing on this very small part. After some practice, I was able to do it while on the full run or when I was rushed for time. I should have said, "Treat me like a child. Make it very simple and start at the most basic step." It is unfortunate that many coaches do not teach these core skills but rather rush into advanced playing before these skills are developed.

TOM BYER AND INFOLDING

Based on his observations, Tom Byer had developed a plan for soccer excellence. His idea was that children should learn very basic skills with the ball. These included stopping and starting, changing direction at different angles, using both feet, pulling the ball back and forth with the sole of the feet, and cutting and turning with both the inside and outside of both feet. In a way, Byer sees the body as the base and a skill as an extension of a person's body. Let's think a little bit about what the function of our feet is. Of course, we use our feet for walking and running. We also use them to climb stairs, to accelerate and use the brakes on a car, to pedal a bike, and to climb a ladder. Each of these actions requires us to coordinate our feet in slightly different ways. However, they are using the existing structure of our feet and extending it. Although ladders, cars, and bikes were not around when humans first began to use their feet, there were natural versions of this. Humans can climb hills, walk on rocks and through water, and jump off a short elevation. Our human world is built as an extension of these "natural" uses of our foot.

Thinking about this more deeply, we can see that Byer's exercises are built on the idea of an adaptation. Rather than thinking about soccer as a skill to be learned, Byer is thinking about soccer as an emergent function. He notes that soccer is a game of passing and shooting. However, basic control has to come first. Then as time goes on, players can learn to pass and shoot.

FROM SPORTS TO SCHOOL

The interesting thing about sports is that we often think about them as physical skills. Sure, there is a mental part, but most people focus on mental toughness and other tactical techniques. In the afterword of Byer's book, Dr. John J. Ratey, an associate professor at Harvard Medical School, takes it one step further. He discusses work from his own book, *Spark: The Revolutionary New*

Science of Exercise and the Brain, which focuses on how physical activity helps skill learning in school.

A brief side note here. Realize that what is increasingly cut out of school is physical activity. Many children are expected to sit quietly for hours on end.

Ratey pushes back against this neglect of our bodies. He notes that the brain is a part of an organism and requires nutrition and care. You might recall the discussion of glia and how it is involved in supporting the brain. He also notes that Naperville High School implemented the principles of brain function into their educational programs. They had students take PE classes regularly. This was especially true for classes where students struggle. What the school accomplished was extraordinary. They were able to improve students' scores and place them on par in some cases with those seen in international scholarship competitions.

The fact that the physical nurturing of our brains helps us in learning new skills provides a very different view on learning. Rather than separating the physical from the mental, it requires us to see these aspects as very well integrated. In the next chapter, we expand on this link more fully. We also move beyond just skills learned in childhood to understanding how childhood skills build more advanced skills. We will move from the tracking of faces—something that infants do from the moment they are born—to reading something that is learned much later in school and then to the way we learn new words. By tracing the path from very early learning to much later learning, we can begin to understand how skills fold in on themselves from infancy all the way to adulthood. This approach also gives insight into how as adults we might take on new skills. Rather than thinking of them as new, we might consider them as a kind of rebirth or rekindling.

FACES, READING, AND THE ROAD TO NEW SKILLS

EMERGENCE, REORGANIZATION, AND COGNITIVE HABITATS

In an episode of the Fox Network show *The Resident*, a neurosurgical trainee and an emergency doctor are stuck in a room after a tornado has ripped up parts of a hospital. They encounter a patient with a severe skull fracture. With no proper surgical tools, the young trainee has to conduct brain surgery, which she does with the help of construction tools. A regular drill is used to open a hole in the patient's skull. A cauterizing iron is used to burn a piece of the patient's brain and stop the bleeding. Pieces of bone fragments from the hole that was drilled are removed with pliers. The toolbox normally used for wires, doors, and pipes is adapted to humans.

The use of tools made for one purpose but adapted for another is a theme that crops up over and over again in the skill-learning literature. Many of the most advanced types of cognition that we undertake—reading, playing chess, sports, and playing an instrument while reading sheet music—are not entirely new. Rather than grow a new area or develop an entirely new skill, our brains use a much more ingenious trick: they take what we can already do and then adapt it to new purposes.

One of the most important skills that we have developed as humans revolves around literacy. Before the advent of writing systems, humans had to communicate all information verbally. Everyday mundane communication did not require much in the way of written words. However, more complex forms of learning required personal attention. For example, in order to learn a highly complex skill like carpentry or sculpture, one would have to work side by side with another person. Our personal history, the story of a particular group of people, and the important information that had to be transmitted from one generation to another required someone to become the storyteller. Through these elaborate stories in the oral tradition, a collective memory could be sustained across generations.

All of this became easier the moment we began to read and write. Reading allows us to off-load our memory, to fly to destinations that are out of reach, and to stretch our minds beyond the limit of what is possible. It is a human skill and it does not appear spontaneously. We must learn to read and we must learn to do it with written material. It is based on language but is not like language. The divide happens around schooling. Whereas humans will create a way to communicate on their own, reading requires some form of instruction. It does not happen on its own when two people meet. The fact that reading does not occur spontaneously and that it involves instruction makes one think that it has no connection to the body. It is the ultimate mental act.

In recent years, Stanislas Dehaene, one of the most influential voices in understanding how the brain adapts to reading, has proposed that reading involves what he has termed *neuronal recycling*. Neuronal recycling is based on the idea that the brain takes what already exists in its toolbox and then reconfigures or rebuilds it.

The idea of recycling is a different way to talk about the emergent aspects of skill learning that lead to mastery. It is similar to the ideas of John Stuart Mill, who posited a chemical transformation whereby hydrogen and oxygen become water. Teilhard de Chardin hints at cognitive transformations by considering the route from pre-life to life to human culture. Each of these goes from the basic elements to complex ones that transformed our planet. In the case of reading, we see a similar transformation. The very beginning of this process is one that is present in many animals from the moment they are born. It is the system used by a chick to recognize its mommy.

WHO'S YOUR MOMMY

In the cartoon short "That's My Mommy" from the show *Tom and Jerry*, a duck egg ends up under the cat named Tom by mistake. By the time Tom notices that the egg is under him, it is already hatching as he looks on puzzled by what has just happened. The duckling looks up at Tom and states, "That's my mommy" (hence the title).

At first Tom is annoyed by the duckling that keeps following him around. Then it dawns on him that a fowl that is fond of him might actually make the perfect dinner dish. Tom proceeds to fatten up the duckling and then finds ways to try and cook him. When Tom places the duckling in an oven, Jerry, the devious mouse that is always ruining Tom's plans, saws a hole in the oven door so that the duckling can escape. The rest of the episode continues with scenes where Jerry keeps rescuing the duckling, who insists on following Tom everywhere because Tom is the duckling's mommy.

After continuously saving the duck, Jerry finally devises a plan so that he can stop rescuing Tom's future dinner. Jerry shows the duckling a book in the hopes that he will learn the concept of mother and child. The book has two opposite pages, each with a mother and offspring. On one page is a mother duck with a duckling, and on the opposite page is a mother cat with a kitten. Jerry points at each page to show the duckling that each animal has its own mommy. Cats with kittens and ducks with ducklings. The duckling follows Jerry's gaze carefully, staring at the duck and then at the cat. He goes between the pages slowly, pausing at the duck and duckling momentarily. Then he immediately turns to the page with the cat, points at her, and declares, "That's my mommy."

Jerry's attempts to save the duckling fail. This leaves Tom, the cat, to use the duckling's strong attachment to hatch his final plan. Tom prepares a recipe for a stew and convinces the duckling to climb up a long spoon that is perched on a pot of boiling water. He looks over at a cookbook that is next to the pot. He slowly reads the recipe, realizing that he is the duck that will be boiled for Tom's sake. He must sacrifice himself for his mommy, and he begins to climb up the spoon. He reaches the top, looks at the boiling pot, and then jumps in.

Before he can fall in the water, Tom reaches over and catches him as tears flow down his cheeks. In the final scene, Jerry fears that Tom's plan has been successful when he finds no sign of the duckling. He then looks out a back window in the kitchen overlooking a creek. In the creek, we see Tom pretending to quack as the duckling follows along in the shallow water behind him. The story is full of subtext, the kind of subtext that went completely over my head when I watched it as a child.

Although in this case it appears in a cartoon, the ability to recognize an object at birth applies not just to animals but also to humans. In animals, the ability to recognize an object at birth has been called *imprinting*.

FOLLOW THE LEADER

Termed *filial imprinting*—or *imprinting* for short—this phenomenon was originally discovered over five hundred years ago by Sir Thomas More. In the 1800s, Douglass Spaulding and later Oskar Heinroth reintroduced it as a topic of research. This renewed interest fit right in with Konrad Lorenz's interest when he was working with Heinroth.

Konrad Lorenz being followed by a group of young geese. *Alamy.*

Lorenz was the one who brought it to public consciousness with the publication of his paper "The Companion in the Environment of Birds" in 1935. Here we can see a picture of Lorenz being pursued by a group of chicks that are imprinted with him as their "mommy."

Lorenz was deeply interested in how animals come to know things. Along with Nikolas Tinbergen, Lorenz advanced a simple question: how do animals know to do things when there is little opportunity to learn it? I had a similar thought with Milo, a goldendoodle that my daughter Kamille convinced us to buy during the COVID-19 pandemic in the summer of 2020. Milo spent his first eight weeks around his mother and sisters. Then he moved in with us. Since then, he has spent pretty much all his time with our family. Occasionally, he has gone to day camp and at times he runs into other dogs. The types of rituals of sniffing each other, bowing down, and then chasing each other were very interesting. It is hard to think that this is all learned. But if it is, who taught Milo to act this way? And why do the other dogs follow suit so easily?

The work of Lorenz and Tinbergen made me think about the possibility that these behaviors are so adaptive that they travel in some inherited form from generation to generation.

Tinbergen argued that many behaviors are instincts, something that is set up in the animals without much information from the outside world. Like my experience with Milo, much of this work on innate principles assumed that adult animals could not have learned these behaviors.

To really pin down that a behavior is innate, it is important to show that it occurs early in life within very specific periods. Lorenz established that imprinting occurred in very specific time windows. Tinbergen and Lorenz stood strongly in favor of a strict dividing line between things that were innate and present at birth and those that were learned.

Most of the skills we learn in life are learned: sports, games like chess, and school subjects such as math and reading. As we become adults these skills become even more refined. Compared to other animals we are experts at learning new skills. Despite all these advanced skills, we come to this world with only a few abilities. In fact, when it comes to vision, we start with a human version of imprinting.

HUMAN IMPRINTING

Unlike birds, newborn humans will not be able to follow their parents around until a few months after birth. The simple fact is that human and bird newborns are different organisms with different needs. Nevertheless, there are some remnants of an imprinting system in humans. A chance observation and a follow-up study provided the first step toward understanding the imprinting system in humans.

In 1975, Carolyn Goren, Merrill Sarty, and Paul Wu had been observing that newborns would stare at the faces of their caregivers for quite a long time. This gave them the idea to test whether newborns might have a preference for faces. They asked parents who were expecting a child in the near future whether it would be OK to perform a small test.

They tested forty newborns after an average of nine minutes after birth. Each of them saw four different paddles that varied from very face-like to less face-like to blank. One of the four was placed in front of each newborn and then moved from left to right. Across all infants, the amount of head turning and eye turning was greatest for the paddles that were more face-like. The less face-like a paddle was, the shorter the distance an infant would track it. When they were shown a paddle that was completely blank, infants showed the least head and eye turning. These results demonstrated that newborns could track face-like visual images more than those that are not face-like. Later work by Mark Johnson and his colleagues was able to show that the initial effect of tracking faces appears in newborns, continues for about a month, and then fades away.

How do we interpret these findings? Johnson and his colleagues interpret their findings to fit within Lorenz and Tinbergen's two-stage theory of imprinting. Early in development, infants use an innate system that leads humans to pay attention to faces. However, this system is there for only a short time. Hence, even though humans have systems that point them toward important objects in the outside world, the influence of these innate systems fades away quickly. Taken together these results confirm that face tracking appears only within a relatively short window after birth.

The second point that is also important to consider is that early face tracking is handled by a brain system that is buried in subcortical areas. Areas below the cortex develop earlier in life and help to guide both sensory and motor processing during these stages. In other words, there is something about faces that allows us to look at how development proceeds for something that we can all agree is innate. Because it is a skill present at birth, it represents a clear way for us to understand how nature and nurture work together.

The final important point is that the eyes and heads of newborns follow a face-like card right at birth. The sensory part is the visual recognition. The motor part is the tracking of the faces. Newborns very quickly begin to track other things that move around them. Thus, face recognition at birth is an entry into the larger realm of figuring out what is moving and where it is moving. The ability to move our eyes to track objects is paramount to learning skills in both athletic and academic settings.

THE IMPORTANCE OF MOVEMENT

In an earlier chapter, we described Piaget's theory of development. His idea was that infants start out with a few basic instincts and then use them to build more complex thinking. The idea that humans are born with only a few basic reflexes got a lot of pushback from researchers. In a way, the finding that infants can track faces goes against Piaget's theory. It is more than a reflex since tracking occurs for faces more than other types of visual objects.

It turns out that movement appears in human fetuses even before birth. Coordinated movements such as yawning, sucking, opening and closing the mouth, and breathing movements can be seen two months after conception. At eighteen to twenty weeks, fetuses can be seen sucking their thumbs. At this age, they also vary their movements. A fetus will move smoothly when the thumb approaches the eyes. When the thumb is put in the mouth, it moves more quickly. These spontaneous movements are the beginning of coordinated actions that will continue in the first few months of life.

Piaget appears to be wrong in his timing. The reflexes appear even before birth. As a neo-Piagetian, I try to look more at the spirit of Piaget's views. Essentially, we start with something simple and then we build from there. Along with being able to track faces, newborns are sensitive to other types of visual information. They are sensitive to emotional expressions in faces. They are also sensitive to motion.

In a very intriguing experiment conducted in 2008, Francesca Simion, Lucia Regolin, and Hermann Bulf from the University of Padua in Italy showed newborn humans a video of a walking hen.

They used what are called *point-light displays*, in which a single dot is placed on specific joints. Previous work had found that chicks are sensitive to this type of movement. When they showed these same videos to newborn humans, the researchers found a preference for these videos of natural biological motion over random motion. That is, the newborns looked longer at the points on a moving hen than at points that moved randomly. They also found that infants looked longer when the video was of an upright hen as opposed to an upside-down hen.

The importance of motion continues from the viewpoint of looking. At around six weeks of age, infants begin to track moving objects. At first their eyes move in jumps that experts call *saccades*. By fourteen weeks of age, most infants begin to follow each object with continuous eye movements. Researchers call these movements *smooth pursuit*. These smooth eye movements reveal that infants are able to predict where an object will move. In this way, they are able to start moving their eyes to a location before the object is there.

PITCH RECOGNITION

The importance of eye movements can also be seen in sports. In baseball, the ability to track a small hard ball that can travel at speeds faster than cars in everyday traffic is paramount. The ball can be thrown at speeds up to 100 miles per hour from a mound 60 feet 6 inches (18.4 meters) away at a height around 10 inches (roughly 25 centimeters). The ball leaves a pitcher's arm at 79–95 miles per hour (122–147 kilometers per hour). The batter has about 75 milliseconds to hit the ball. Because time is short, a batter has to recognize the ball before it arrives. The batter will also have to initiate a swing when the ball is halfway between the mound and the plate. Baseball players are like newborn infants who must guess where the ball will be before it gets there.

Professional baseball players are known for inventing all kinds of interesting ways to practice batting. Barry Bonds, one of the greatest hitters of all time and the holder of the home run record in Major League Baseball, was known to practice with his father Bobby using balls with numbers. Barry did not just hit balls. He would hit balls and call out the numbers while he was hitting them. The idea was to get him to focus on the number on the ball while he was hitting.

I can name hitting a baseball as one of the skills that came more easily to me. As a child, I loved baseball. I remember listening to the San Francisco Giants on the radio. That is what we did before the explosion of TV channels that brought every game into our living rooms—or any room for that matter, if we so wish. One year I listened to almost every game for most of the month of July. I also got to see a few baseball games live and was overwhelmed by how large the baseball field was and the way the stadium surrounded you. It was like no other feeling I had ever had.

Inspired by the great baseball players of the time, my friends and I would play sandlot baseball using a tennis ball to try and soften the impact on our neighbors. When seventh grade came, I grew excited and nervous to think about team tryouts. In anticipation of tryouts, I took time to work on my hitting stroke using a Johnny Bench Batter Up. Johnny Bench, a catcher for the Cincinnati Reds, was known for being a great batter. His batter up was a big tire that was filled with cement and had a pole in the middle. Around the pole was a contraption that spun in a circle. I would hit balls on my batter up every day for a few months before my big day.

When the big day arrived, our baseball coach had us try different drills in which we caught and threw the ball to one another. On the second day, he put us to bat and had us hit a few balls. Then miraculously I found I could hit the ball pretty well. I had a few advantages that had gone unnoticed. Even though I was pretty slow and not particularly well conditioned, I had very good eyesight. I found this out many years later when I saw that my eyesight was getting worse in my late forties. I told the optometrist that I could not see as well as I once had. When she gave me an eye test, I found out it was 20/15. So, my eyesight was not bad. It was just not as good as it had been in early adulthood. My guess is that I must have had 20/10 or maybe even better. With this amazing eyesight, I could see the ball early, and that gave me a jump on the ball relative to others who could not see as well.

If my eyesight could give me an advantage, I can only imagine what a very good hitter would manage. A professional baseball player typically has 20/12 vision, and some players actually wear contacts in order to get to that level. Imagine what a professional baseball player has in his arsenal.

Barry Bonds must have seen the ball so early after hitting millions of balls in his lifetime. In a way, great hitters read the ball and the pitcher, and react in a way that great chess players do. They are able to process information much more quickly than nonexperts do.

PITCHING THE BOYS INTO THEIR PLACE

With all the practice with such extreme conditions, one would think that baseball players could hit any moving object thrown at them. Think again. As David Epstein notes in his book *The Sports Gene*, being good at one type of motion tracking does not make baseball players good at all types of motion tracking.

In 2004, a group of baseball players who felt they had the upper hand in terms of their ability to track a moving object got caught in a trap. Jenny Finch, a pitcher on the American Olympic team at the time, challenged them to hit softballs. Softball has three major differences from baseball in terms of pitching: First, the mound, the raised dirt portion on which a pitcher stands when hurling the ball at the batter, is closer in softball than it is baseball. Second, the softball itself is much larger than a baseball. Finally, the ball is thrown underhand rather than overhand like it is in baseball.

With his heightened place in the hierarchy of sports, the male professional baseball player feels he can compete with any pitcher in the world. With this mindset the group of baseball players approached hitting a softball thrown by a woman with enthusiasm. They thought they would smoke the *girl* pitcher hurling the much bigger softball.

They were wrong! The woman softball pitcher mowed through all the batters. They could barely lay a bat on the ball. Even Barry Bonds, who had practiced with numbers and hit many, many home runs, could barely manage to tap a ball into foul territory.

In softball, these men would not have made the first cut. Rather than playing softball they would most likely have been relegated to the position of water boy. In this sport, the women reigned supreme.

Seeing baseballs or softballs move in space and then meeting them with a bat is a task that builds on our basic abilities. Like face perception it involves the recombination of small skills into a specialized larger skill. The skill becomes so specialized that it almost becomes inflexible. And thus, we have grown men being dragged down into the abyss of missed swing after missed swing by a woman who is hurling a much larger ball at a much closer distance.

Like tracking faces and moving balls, reading also involves active motion. In the case of reading, our eyes have to move across a line to capture letters, words, and sentences. The interesting part is that reading is, as I noted earlier, something we learn in school. Thus, reading words and pitches may be more related than it might appear on the surface.

Reading in some way is like tracking a moving object like a ball that is thrown at us and that has to be hit. As we move across the page, our eyes shift from one word to the other. The shifts are followed by moments during which the word is being read. These moments are called *fixations* by researchers.

Research on eye fixations in children beginning to learn how to read parallels that of the object-tracking literature. Basically, at very early stages of reading, children's eyes move in a much more sporadic manner. They jump from one word to the other slowly. Children also fixate on a word for much longer than adults. As children read more and more, they begin to approximate adult reading. Their eyes move forward more quickly and they are able to anticipate which word is coming next. They can use context to speed up their reading even more.

So far we have seen that expert readers are like object trackers. They learn to move their eyes to coordinate the movements needed to read words. This leaves us with two questions: What happens as a person becomes an expert who looks at particular types of objects? How does expertise get wired up in our brains?

KANWISHER'S FFA

I hate acronyms. You might have thought the title of this section was referring to the Future Farmers of America or the Forum Fisheries Agency. The FFA I am talking about is just below those other two in popularity. One of the *F*'s is for "face" and the other is for "area." In this case, FFA refers to the fusiform face area. The fusiform gyrus lies internally at the very bottom of the brain. The fusiform gyrus is broadly an area that stretches from the occipital cortex in the back of the brain to the very lowest parts of the temporal cortex. The story of the FFA goes back to the mid-1990s, when Nancy Kanwisher, a professor at MIT, had the opportunity use a new form of MRI to scan the brain. fMRI uses a souped-up MRI scanner to map brain function indirectly. When neurons in a brain area fire, blood begins to flow to that area. When it flows to an area, that blood is oxygen rich. fMRI uses this change to help pin down what areas are more active when we are shown pictures, words, sounds, or any other kind of stimuli that might interest us.

Other methods fit in with Kanwisher's ideas. Robert Desimone and colleagues had focused on the fusiform gyrus area. The results showed that single cells in this region would respond more strongly to some visually presented images than others. For example, some cells were more sensitive to hands than to faces. Others were more sensitive to faces than hands. Positron emission tomography (PET) used a very mild radioactive tracer that had also been used with humans. Two studies, one led by Sergent and another led by Haxby, had found brain activity in the lower part of the temporal lobe—which includes the fusiform gyrus—when participants looked at faces compared to other stimuli.

Kanwisher used the information from earlier studies when designing her first study with this method. She put herself in the scanner and then looked to see if she would get the same area of activity across multiple testing sessions. She did. The particular cluster of neurons sensitive to faces appeared over and over again. This led her to simply look at this area across multiple subjects. Her studies have firmly established the fusiform face area as an area devoted to the processing of faces.

One question that naturally comes up is whether the FFA is part of a system that we learn or whether we are born with it. Newer work does give us evidence of responses to faces in the fusiform gyrus in infants between two and nine months old. In other words, the FFA appears very early in life but not at birth. This suggests that it might result from the innate system set up to track faces early in life.

This leaves us with a natural question. Does the FFA respond just to faces? Or can this area be "recycled" to handle other functions? This was the question that intrigued another researcher interested in faces, Isabel Gauthier.

GAUTHIER'S GREEBLES AND VISUAL RECYCLING

The story of the FFA and the work of Kanwisher came about the time Gauthier was completing her dissertation at Yale. Gauthier's main idea is that face processing is special because it represents a form of visual expertise. Findings from the expertise literature suggested that people who become good at a very specific category of visual objects—such as judges for dog shows or expert birdwatchers—begin to show effects that are similar to those seen in the face recognition literature. Gauthier found that if she trained undergraduates to look at alien-looking Greebles they behaved like dog experts with dogs and like other humans with faces.

Gauthier suggests that becoming a visual expert has to do with how the FFA gets wired up over time. Basically, if we look at a category enough times, we will eventually become an expert. If we become an expert, then the FFA will fire for these newly formed categories. Research carried out by Gauthier and her collaborators fits right in with this view. Other researchers have also found that dog experts will show activity in the FFA for dogs. The same happens for car experts. However, when people are shown an object for which they are not an expert, there is no corresponding FFA activity.

Gauthier's work suggests that the FFA is the result of expertise developed over time. If we were aliens, and our parents' faces looked like Greebles, then we would have an FGA—a fusiform greeble area. Similarly, if we grew up looking only at cars, birds, or dogs, we would develop FCAs, FBAs, and FDAs. I know I hate acronyms, but this hammers in Gauthier's point. It is the act of seeing a category over and over again that makes us experts.

As noted earlier, there is another way to interpret these data so they fit in more nicely with emergentism and the idea of neuronal recycling. All the visual categories that we form in our brains spring from the very simple primal sketch that we make of faces in the very first minutes of our lives. As we track faces for the first one or two months in a fairly simple way, we are actually in a way training the cortex for what is to come. As time passes, we begin to look at many different types of objects. Over the first few years of our lives, we create a well-developed visual category recognition system that can handle faces and other objects. This sets the stage for more and more complex types of processing.

FROM INFANT TO ADULT PATTERN RECOGNITION

The idea of neuronal recycling as proposed by Dehaene argues that many of our complex higher skills use our basic mental tools and then adapt them for other uses. In the brain, the basic tools for reading are based on sensorimotor building blocks. It involves linking what we see with what we hear. And here is where face and object perception become interesting. The early systems that detect faces consist of brain areas that link what an infant sees with an area involved in movement. In short, putting what we hear and see together is fundamentally important to us as humans.

You could think of reading as using a different type of audiovisual detector. In the case of reading, we are linking letters that are visual with the sounds that letters and their combinations make. Not surprisingly, the link ends up involving an area of the brain—the fusiform gyrus—that Dehaene calls the *visual word form area*, or VWFA. This VWFA appears very close to the fusiform face area, which is devoted to specialization for faces.

The specialization of faces proceeds from subcortical to cortical areas in the fusiform gyrus. As object recognition proceeds across time, it becomes more and more specialized. Thus, areas that are devoted to object recognition and form a bridge between sights and sounds are recycled, leading to a VWFA.

In addition to building up specialized visual ability, expert recognition relies on specialized tracking systems. In the case of tracking pitches, eye movements learn to anticipate where the ball will be even when it is thrown very quickly. Our eyes also learn to track words by using movement.

Reading also builds on the language system by using all the sound combinations that are built up during early childhood and then adding a written script on top of it. Just as language takes pieces of sound, binds them together, and creates a greater whole out of very basic parts, reading adds more to the system. If language is a new machine built of old parts, reading adds a turbo-charged engine to the process.

There is one small problem with the machine analogy. Building assumes a construction, an artificial putting together of things that are not naturally available. Reading, like all our higher-level mental abilities, is not manufactured. These abilities grow. We might say that reading is more biological. It is the product of a combination and recombination of processes that were already lying around in our cognitive ecosystem. It is the ultimate testament to how we are able to learn new things by repurposing existing abilities meant to do something else.

8

CASE STUDY: HOW JANE AND GAVIN USE MOTION TO RECOGNIZE THE UNRECOGNIZABLE

JANE'S SECRET

Valerie Jane Morris-Goodall was born in 1934 in Hampstead, London. In her autobiography, *Reason for Hope*, Jane Goodall, the professional name she later took, reflects on her own journey as a primatologist. She describes her childhood as idyllic, but not in the economic sense because her family did not live a life filled with travel or great luxuries. Goodall says that her family could not buy a car or a bicycle, or take any fancy trips to distant lands. Despite this economic hardship, her family had everything they needed, enough food to eat, and a roof over their heads. With the very positive spin that she always placed on things, she describes her childhood as one filled with warmth and laughter, giving her an appreciation for life and the interconnectedness of things. She grew up with her sister Judy, who was exactly four years younger than her, in a household that cherished but did not squash her with religion. They did not have to attend church or say grace at every meal. However, they did have to say their prayers every night, and they were taught the importance of basic values such as courage, honesty, compassion, and tolerance. Goodall also played outside a lot and enjoyed learning about nature.

This allowed her to gain a spiritual awareness in a manner similar to Ramón y Cajal, who enjoyed playing outside and eventually spent hours sketching out neurons.

Goodall's father also bore resemblance to Ramón y Cajal's father Ramón Casus, who learned to live a life without much luxury. She states, "Because every penny mattered, everything that was extra such as an ice cream, a journey on a train, a cinema, was a treat, exciting, to be remembered. If only everyone could be blessed with such a childhood. How different, I believe, the world would be."

She goes on to describe her life mystically as one that involved people and a larger being who guided her along her unusual path. Most important was her mother, who gave her confidence and allowed her to love nature. From a young age Goodall loved animals despite growing up in London and later moving just outside the city. Sometime after her first birthday, her father, Mortimer Goodall, who worked as an engineer in London, bought her a stuffed chimpanzee. Many of the family friends thought a young child might be scared of such an "ugly" creature. Goodall loved and cherished her Jubilee so much that all the stuffed animal's fur wore off. This love for animals kept her company during her childhood in the young group of earthworms she wanted to take into bed. Her interest in animals continued as she grew older. One particularly interesting memory of hers revolved around hens and how they laid eggs. Young Goodall wondered how a hen had a hole big enough to lay an egg. To find out she waited until a chick entered the henhouse. Once inside she followed the hen around to see how she laid her eggs. Of course, the hen ran away from her. So Goodall decided to hide in a corner very quietly. Eventually, a hen came over, laid an egg, and then tapped it with her claw.

Her love of animals continued through adolescence and into adulthood when Dr. Louis Leakey invited her to Gombe Stream National Park, where she began to work with chimpanzees. She was so talented that Leakey sent her back to Cambridge, where she enrolled in a PhD program. Goodall continued her work and eventually became more involved in helping to address a number of political issues that were intertwined with the need to protect animals. This began in earnest in 1986. For one seven-week tour she began to tally up all her work: 71 lectures, 32 airplanes, and 170 media interviews. One would think that a campaign like this could only be undertaken by someone who enjoyed the company of people.

However, despite all her success during a storied career, Goodall carried a secret. She enjoyed people's company but always dreaded one particular aspect of these encounters. Over the years, she noticed that she had difficulty remembering people's faces. She always assumed that it was some form of mental laziness. For some people, it was easier to recognize faces. They might have a distinguishable characteristic, such as a mole or a scar. Others might be very beautiful or have a unique nose. But for the vast majority of people her strategies of looking for distinctive features did not work. She would often not recognize people even though she had met them the day before. She found herself continually apologizing to everyone.

She confessed this secret to Oliver Sacks, a well-known neuropsychologist. Sacks confirmed that he had the same malady and that his was worse. At least Goodall could recognize loved ones and found ways to recognize people she was around often. To Sacks, every person was a stranger. He could not recognize their faces. Goodall found out she had prosopagnosia, a condition whose name comes from the Greek words *prosopon* ("face") and *agnosia* ("lack of knowledge"). This syndrome has a more popular name, *face blindness*. The history of prosopagnosia, its discovery, and how it takes us into a modern debate about the nature of human knowledge is one of the most interesting topics that gets at an ability that we all have but that gets built up with very small parts that are assembled and reassembled across time.

GAVIN'S SECRET

On the surface, Jane Goodall and Gavin Newsom have little in common. One is a scientist, the other a politician. She is English and he is a Californian. He spends his days figuring out how to run a state that could be its own country both politically and geographically. She advocates for a better world. She doesn't have to worry about getting reelected or whether her ideals might get her voted out of office. He doesn't have to worry about constituents a continent away that have no voice and no power. However, they are both unable to recognize objects that others recognize easily.

Gavin Christopher Newsom was born in San Francisco, California, on October 10, 1967. A fourth-generation San Franciscan, he comes from a storied family. His father was a state appeals court judge and an attorney for Getty Oil. On his mother's side, his great-grandfather, Scotsman Thomas Addis, was a pioneering scientist in the field of nephrology and a professor of medicine at Stanford University. Joanna Newsom, his second cousin, is a musician.

As a child, Newsom struggled at school. Initially, he was placed into a French-English bilingual school but transferred due to his difficulty with reading. His difficulties did not subside in an English-only school. To overcome his difficulties, he used other methods to learn the material, including audio recordings.

As with Goodall, his difficulties in recognition did not transfer over to visual processing in general. Goodall never had any problems with written words. Newsom had no problem with tracking baseballs. His skills were good enough to earn him a scholarship at Santa Clara University. Unfortunately, his pitching skills dropped off after two years and he had to leave baseball altogether.

Newsom became a successful businessman, founding a company that contained twenty-three businesses including wineries, hotels, and restaurants. As a politician, he worked hard to overcome his reading difficulties. However, his dyslexia is very severe. Even today as an adult, he has trouble pronouncing words. He needs to circle words and underline them to make sure that he stays on the same line. His struggles became so great that he went on to write a book for children that might be helped by hearing his story.

SENSORIMOTOR SOLUTIONS

Across several sections in this book, we have considered the importance of emergence, understanding how skills are combined and recombined across time. In the cases of Jane Goodall and Gavin Newsom, we can see that there are times when a transformation does not take place. We might think of this as a deficiency. Certainly, both of them felt the effects of this. Goodall lacked the ability to learn people's faces and Newsom lacked the ability to recognize words easily.

We can, however, take another view here. Rather than thinking about how they were *not* able to recognize things, let's think about how they *were* able to recognize things. To overcome their limitations, each of them invoked additional backup skills. Goodall would focus on particular features that might identify a person. She would guide her eyes in a different way. When forced to read, Newsom would physically work on learning the words. He would make his body act differently by underlining and circling words. There is indeed a lesson here for those learning a new skill. Part of it relies on recognition and the other part on action.

There is one final interesting point. Neither Jane nor Gavin has a documented language problem. In fact, Gavin prefers listening and speaking to reading and writing. As we will see next, the importance of hearing in language, which appears very early in life, is a skill that follows most of us for the rest of our lives.

9

THE LONG ROAD TO ADULT LANGUAGE ACQUISITION

EMBRACING DISRUPTION?

We often marvel at children's ability to learn language. The timeline in very brief format runs like this: Children are born. At birth, they are able to recognize their mother's voice. They seem to have a preference for sounds from their native language. A few months later, they begin to babble. Young infants can recognize the sounds of foreign languages. However, within a year, the window closes. Around a year after birth, it is apparent that they have what is called *symbolic representation*. Even though many eleven-month-olds cannot speak, they can actually make small signs. For example, just before her first birthday, my daughter Kiara, the earliest speaker of my kids, would hold her hand up and wave while saying, "Gaba-gabye." Between one and two years of age, children's language skills keep expanding. They produce single words, then two-word combinations, and then *boom*.

The boom is the virtual sound of a multiword explosion. Sometime around their second birthday, children begin to speak in basic sentences. By three years of age, they have been branded as a grammatical genius. At five they are in school learning to read and write. My friend Plinio Junqueira de Schmidt, a Brazilian I met many years ago, used to joke that the most intimidating thing for him was skiing in Germany. The German children not only skied better but they were better at German than him. Philosophy had driven him to learn German, and there were not a lot of ski slopes in Brazil. One day on the ski slopes he realized that he was in a race he had already lost.

If you are like most people trying to learn a language, you might relate to Plinio. It seems like a daunting task to learn a language later in life. Sometimes you feel like you should not even try. Let me start by saying that you have every right to be intimidated. When I was in Germany, I remember feeling sweat pour down my arm. It wasn't from running around chasing a tennis ball in the Texas heat. It was whenever I had to try and follow a conversation with a group of Germans on a very cold day outside. Aside from trying to stay warm, I was busy trying to keep up. I was trying to avoid having them switch to English because I wanted to keep practicing German. I suppose the stress made me a bit less cold than I would have been otherwise.

In chapter 7, we looked at face processing as a way to understand at a very basic level the ways in which our brain handles special categories. We saw how early-specialized systems help newborns to track a face. Later-developing systems begin to extract more and more information out of faces. The presence of these special categories both in our behavior and in our brains leads to a second question. This second question revolves around whether these special categories are present at birth. In the case of face processing, there is clear evidence that infants will track a face minutes after being born.

However, face processing does not stop at birth with the tracking of faces. This early-developing system deeper in the subcortex just points us in the right direction. Later, the outer layer of the brain, the cortex, takes over. Our brains shift from faces to objects. Eventually objects are recognized, and later these objects are linked to their corresponding sounds. Thus, object recognition becomes word recognition. The most important point is that very small differences, focusing on faces, result in much more complex later-developing cognitive machinery.

Like face recognition and word recognition later, language also begins from a simple system dedicated to sounds. Later it takes on more complex forms as we get older. The intention here is to put language in its proper place within the ecosystem that marks the boundaries of our cognitive habitat. After all, language is perhaps the most advanced sensorimotor skill ever to grace this planet.

THE MUSIC OF LANGUAGE

Like playing tennis, learning multiple languages is a feat that seems to defy the laws that govern human achievement. In his book *Babel No More*, Michael Erard discusses hyperpolyglots (super language learners) who are able to learn eleven or more languages. There are three aspects of these gifted language learners. One is that they have an incredible feel for languages. They have a sense of what is right and wrong in each language without thinking about it. Second, they can step out of a language and see the rules as if they were road maps showing how all the rules work, how you form words and sentences, and what the exceptions are. Third, they seem to have a near obsession with languages. Most of them spend their entire day practicing different languages. It is the type of interest that can lead to a career as an applied linguist whose study of languages extends to the study of language as a science.

One interesting facet that Erard discusses is the availability of the languages. According to him, gifted language learners do not have all languages on the tip of their tongue and ready to be used at any time. Rather, they have about four or five base languages that they can speak spontaneously. The other languages are surge languages—they can be spoken only after some practice.

One question that you might ask is, what does a feel for language mean? Katherine Demuth and her colleagues propose that grammar, like dribbling in soccer or serving in tennis, is built from basic physical building blocks. We can think of language as having both notes and a melody. The notes are the actual speech sounds, like the sound of *s* in *speech*. The melody refers to the way in which the words flow together in a spoken sentence. Demuth points to the way in which children take the notes and melody as a starting point and build the language up from that. However, hyperpolyglots learn many of their languages as adults and yet they are able to sound and appear like native speakers. The question that remains is how they are able do that. For the majority of the population, the window to learn a language like a native begins to close in late childhood or early adolescence. How do these hyperpolyglots keep it open so long? And if they can keep it open so long, how might those without this language giftedness be able to do so as well?

One hint at how these language geniuses achieve their feat can be found in the work by Turker and Reiterer. Early in her career Reiterer wondered why learners who were about the same age and had learned a second language at about the same time in late childhood or in early adolescence differed to such a great extent in their accents and their abilities to speak in that language. Her career did not begin with a permanent position; rather, she spent time going from one lab to another. "It was a difficult time," she notes.

It was during this time that she made her keen observation on second-language learners. It was also a time when she found something else that caught her attention. The same people who had a very light accent in their second language were also able to produce sounds in a completely unknown language, also with a lighter accent. Reiterer has spent a good chunk of her career building on these early findings. She suggests that the ability to hear speech sounds and produce unaccented speech forms the core of language aptitude. Like tennis and soccer, language begins with sensorimotor building blocks and then advances to a full-fledged system.

As I noted earlier, young infants are equipped with the ability to recognize a very large number of the different speech sounds produced by speakers of different languages. The window to this ability closes early, and by ten months of age children can recognize only the sounds from their native language. Hence, Japanese adults find it very difficult, if not impossible, to recognize the distinction between *r* and *l* that they could distinguish before they were a year old. However, infants raised in Japan with exposure purely to Japanese can recognize the distinction between *r* and *l*. The idea is that age brings a sharpening of an ability to recognize native-language sounds and a loss in the ability to hear sounds that do not exist in their native language.

My colleague Ping Li told me that every time he presents this work in his class a student will come up afterward and ask him about the window closing at ten months. The student will then go on to say that he or she learned English well after that window closed and yet they have no accent. Studies have shown that the window in the ability to hear speech sounds in another language can be reopened for children who are just over a year old. In principle, the window should not stay open much past two or three years old. However, many of the students that approach Ping learned their second languages much older. How can that be?

The story of how it is that someone can acquire a language in childhood and not have an accent brings us back to the work of Turker and Reiterer. Reiterer has also worked with polyglots—those who speak five or more languages—and compared them to bilinguals and multilinguals. Her view is that polyglots, a softer version of the hyperpolyglots that Erard describes, are intrinsically motivated to learn languages. They may not spend their entire day learning languages, but they take a keen interest, which has led them to learn languages that are not in their immediate environment. Language learning for polyglots is not just due to exposure but to actually having an interest in language.

When she compared polyglots to multilinguals or bilinguals she found that polyglots scored better in language aptitude. Multilinguals and bilinguals did not score any better than monolinguals. We have observed a similar finding in our laboratory, although our findings suggest that the age at which someone learns a language matters. Pilar Archila-Suerte did some work along these lines. She was keenly interested in studying how people learn to process the speech sounds in a language. Her early work looked at the differences between early and late learners of English as a second language along with English monolinguals. These studies found that late learners look different from monolinguals and early learners. Specifically, early learners and monolinguals hear a speech sound in English and recognize it on its own. Late learners, on the other hand, rely more on recognizing the differences between sounds. Particularly hard for Spanish speakers are the vowel sounds in *cup* and *cop*. Pilar found that nonnative English speakers recognized these sounds better when they were placed next to other sounds. Hence, a nonnative English speaker would recognize "cop" better if it was heard after the word "cup." Native speakers and early learners, however, can hear "cop" as "cop" and "cup" as "cup" even when they hear the words alone.

This finding is similar to what is found in music. When most people hear notes, with some training they can learn to identify which notes they are. However, researchers have identified two different processes people use when doing so. For a few people with training, a note can be identified on its own. Thus, people with absolute or perfect pitch can detect a single note in isolation. However, for a much larger segment of the population, a single note is not enough for them to be able to name it. The majority of people use relative pitch, in which they distinguish a note by comparing it to other notes. Likewise, early nonnative English speakers and monolinguals hear each speech sound without having to compare it.

The connection between music and language goes beyond just the way in which single sounds are heard. This connection has really come to the fore through Reiterer's work. As I note above, she observed that polyglots seem to have better language abilities.

A second finding that links music and language is that musical training seems to help in the ability to produce sounds in a foreign language. Reiterer has found that musicians outperform nonmusicians when it comes to producing a nonnative accent. Among musicians, vocalists are the best. Those who sing can sound more native-like in a foreign language than those who do not. In short, spoken language seems to be built from the little parts of sound that also help to build music. So the core of music and language is based on sound, but over time they take two different paths. As the paths diverge they begin to combine and recombine to become something very different. In language, we begin to learn that groups of sounds are mapped into single items that have meaning that we call words. The words become their own things that combine with other words in particular combinations using grammatical rules. Like the tennis serve and the accompanying strokes, we get simple parts that when combined and recombined become a much greater whole. At the most advanced levels, the game of tennis, a piano concerto, and a poem take on greater significance than anyone would have anticipated when looking at the very beginning of the process of creating them. It is reflective of the emergence of skill that occurs on our road to mastery.

The question that naturally arises is what happens to all the people with nonnative accents. Is it really the case that they cannot learn languages as well? Does accent equal language? Whereas Reiterer suggests this might be the case, there has to be more to it than that. As you will see next, some individuals with very strong accents have no problem with reading and writing.

HOW WOULD YOU LIKE TO WRITE?

In an episode of the TV show *Lost*, Hugo "Hurley" Reyes, a character known for his references to *Star Wars*, gains the ultimate advantage when sent into the past. The show *Lost* was a modern version of *Robinson Crusoe*, the novel in which the eponymous protagonist Crusoe survives all sorts of hardships after being stuck on an abandoned island. As in the 1719 novel, Hurley, along with many other characters, are stuck on an island where they encounter all sorts of unusual phenomena. Season 5 of *Lost* takes a sudden turn with some of the marauders being sent into the past.

Hurley, realizing that he has been transported back to the 1970s, begins writing in his journal feverishly. Taking pen to paper incessantly starts to pique the curiosity of his friends. More and more people start to wonder what is wrong with him. One of the characters finally breaks down and asks Hurley why he is writing so feverishly. He answers that they have gone back to the time before *Star Wars* ever came out. Hurley has taken it upon himself to write the sequel to the original movie *The Empire Strikes Back*. Along the way, he gets rid of some of the parts that he did not like. Instead of George Lucas and Lawrence Kasdan, it will be Hurley who will get the credit.

If you could go back into the past and write a great novel in English, which would it be? There are a lot of good authors out there. You might like the writing of Charles Dickens, Maya Angelou, Xiaolu Guo, or Khaled Hosseini. For me, Joseph Conrad's *Heart of Darkness* takes the prize. Just read the passage below:

> The day was ending in a serenity of still and exquisite brilliance. The water shone pacifically; the sky, without a speck, was a benign immensity of unstained light; the very mist on the Essex marsh was like a gauzy and radiant fabric, hung from the wooded rises inland, and draping the low shores in diaphanous folds. Only the gloom to the west, brooding over the upper reaches, became more sombre every minute, as if angered by the approach of the sun.

Joseph Conrad is actually the anglicized form of Józef Teodor Konrad Korzeniowski. He was not a native speaker of English. In fact, Conrad did not learn English until he was in his twenties. According to his contemporaries, his accent in English was horrid. Yet despite sounding so bad, he wrote so beautifully.

There is a bit of good and bad news in this example. As I noted earlier, the good news is that you don't have to sound like a native to be "good" in a language. The bad news? You may never sound like a native in a language you learn as an adult. My mom has spoken English for almost sixty years. Yet no one would mistake her accent for a lack of knowledge. If like Hurley in *Lost* I was sent into the past before *Heart of Darkness* was written, I would gladly trade my native-sounding accent in English to be able to write like Conrad.

So how did Conrad pull it off? How was he able to write so beautifully in a language that he learned in his twenties? The answer to this question might surprise you.

ENGLISH IS EASY

English has become the lingua franca. It is the language that is used today for commerce, education, music, movies, and so on. The list goes on. There are a lot of reasons for this. Some have argued that it has to do with colonialism. England was a great superpower that had colonies across the world. In fact, a recent article suggests that English gained its prominence because of Sir Winston Churchill. Churchill claimed that Great Britain could come to dominate the world via its language.

If only it were so easy. If it were just a matter of raw numbers, there are at least two other candidate languages that we could consider. Mandarin speakers outnumber English speakers in the world. Spanish native speakers outnumber English native speakers. And yet, when French and Spanish speakers meet, they are as likely to speak English as Spanish. If the two of them meet a Mandarin speaker, English would be the natural choice.

I am sure the Spanish-speaking and Mandarin-speaking leaders have also wanted to dominate the world linguistically. In fact, the list of colonial powers that would have wanted to instill linguistic dominance abounds. If we consider just the more modern European empires, we have the French, the Dutch, the Portuguese, the

Germans, and the Vikings. And yet English lies atop the linguistic perch. Churchill's statements were strong, but intent of language dominance is not enough.

Maybe it is the transfer of power from England to the United States, which has become the dominant economic, political, and cultural force around the globe. Maybe Franklin Delano Roosevelt and Ronald Reagan pushed the English language even further. This is not a book about politics or about global hegemony. Those might be reasons for the language's dominance, but there is another way to think about this issue beyond politics and economics.

Rather than thinking of English as the cause, let's consider a more emergentist way of thinking. English is both cause and effect. As it spread around the world, it changed, and as it changed it spread around the world, and so on and so forth across centuries. It turns out that languages that are spoken more widely around the world become simplified. In the case of English, there are relatively few markings on words. Take the verb *to have*. Only he/she/it uses *has*. All the other pronouns use *have*: I/you/they/we/have. He/she/it has. Compare this to German, which is *Ich habe, du hast, Ihr hat, wir haben, sie/er/es hat.* Oh, and there is a you plural formal, *Sie haben*. Six forms of the verb in German, two in English.

Comparing German and English is interesting because English is a Germanic language. Both languages share a lot of words, like *haben* and *have*. However, the English versions are highly simplified.

It was not always that way. Work looking at English historically has found that it keeps getting simpler. Let's take the verb *to slide*. Because German has many irregular forms, I have started to build up all kinds of forms that do not exist in English. In German, the past progressive is *wir haben geschlitten*, "we have slid." Notice that English has forms like wrote/written and rode/ridden, so why not slid/slidden? To me it should be "we have slidden." Doesn't sound so bad, does it? In fact, *slidden* is an archaic form that was replaced by *slid*. If ever I get transported back to a remote past like Hurley did, I will make sure to use it. Otherwise, here in the present day I am stuck with "we have slid."

If we listen to British English, we have a few more irregular forms. *Lit* instead of *lighted, dreamt* instead of *dreamed, shone* instead of *shined*. English is going completely regular and just adding *-ed* to almost every verb. Research has begun to predict which verbs are likely to be lost.

Aside from Churchill's declarations, there is another reason that Joseph Conrad could write so beautifully in English. He did not have to worry about a lot of these endings. French, which might have been the other lingua franca, suffers from a bunch of endings that have to be learned. Spanish, too. And forget German. There you have all kinds of endings you have to keep track of. *The* in English becomes *der, die*, or *das*, and it changes depending on whether it is the actor, the receiver, or somehow involved indirectly. With little grammar to learn, Conrad could write a sentence in English without worrying about making a mistake.

ENGLISH IS HARD

OK, so now you think that I must be negating everyone's suffering in trying to learn English. English is not possibly that easy. Teenagers who are native speakers spend a lot of time learning vocabulary in high school. How can a nonnative speaker possibly compete?

I remember having to learn a lot of vocabulary words in high school for the Scholastic Aptitude Test (SAT). At one point, I was busy memorizing words. My dad told me that if I learned the Latin and Greek roots, I would do much better because I could then figure out what the words meant. Like all teenagers, I scoffed at my dad's suggestion. I told him there was no way he could figure out what all these words meant. He told me to throw some words at him.

So, I did. Antediluvian. His response: Ante like *antes* in Spanish meant "before" in Latin. Deluvio was a flood. It meant before the flood. I looked down at my book and he was right. OK, maybe he got lucky. Word number two, bacchanalian. My dad said that Bacchus was the Greek god of wine. It must mean festive. I looked down and strike two. I was in trouble. Rather than strike out I decided to walk away. I had listened to my dad and taken one year of Latin. But all I remember is salve magister. Antediluvian and bacchanalian never made it on the map for me.

My dad learned English in his late teens and had a very thick accent. But like Conrad he had an elegant vocabulary. He knew English better than a native speaker. He didn't speak better but he definitely knew better.

Many years later, I finally broke down and began to think more about Latin. It actually happened indirectly for a completely different reason. For the majority of my life, I arrived at a somewhat harmonious state knowing English, Spanish, and Portuguese. Sure, there was some interference and some words were slightly different, but for the most part I could manage all three.

Then I learned German and everything flew out the window. Yes, the grammar is hard, but that was not the hardest part for me. I could not find any words. I literally understood nothing. When I asked my daughter Kiara, "What does *wiederholen* mean?" she responded, "It means 'repeat.'" I asked her how she knew. She responded, "It's common everyday vocabulary." I would only learn later that *wieder* means something like "again." *Holen* is something like "hauling." *Wiederholen* means "to haul again." In other words, repeat. There are bunch of forms like *wiederstarten*, *wiedersprechen*, and *wiederspielen*—start again, speak again, and play again.

As I reflected on my German word-finding problem, I realized that it had one simple cause. I could not fall back on my Romance language tricks. This would be something like repeat, *repetir* and *repetir*. I repeat, *yo repito, eu repito* in English, Spanish, and Portuguese, respectively. In German, *Ich habe es wiedergeholt.* I was lost. The funny thing is that English speakers I met would sometimes say that German is easier than Spanish. That really threw me for a loop. Of course, for them English and German were well Germanic. They were very similar. Not to me.

English has taken another turn, one that started in the year 1000, when the Normans invaded Britain. When this happened,

Norman French became the language of royalty. Back then English was the common language. This distinction still remains today. It explains my word-finding problems. It also explains how Conrad could write so beautifully.

THE LATIN EMPIRE STILL RULES

When I read an article in *Academia Letters* about English's dominance being political, I immediately had another thought. Was it really Churchill who had declared dominance over the world? In fact, it was not English that was dominating academic language across the world. In a way, English was just a vehicle for a much earlier influence. It began when the Normans invaded England and continued as the Roman Empire spread across Europe. In my view, it is the Latin Empire that still rules.

To test this idea, I needed to look at words learned at different ages. I started with the top fifty nouns used by English native speakers in early childhood, in everyday adult English, and academic English. Using different databases, I found that early in childhood the vast majority of the fifty most used words are of Germanic origin. Animals like mouse, cow, and sheep come from German/Old English. Body parts too (hand, arm, feet, mouth). To look at everyday adult vocabulary I looked at which words were used frequently on American soap operas. Here it was fifty-fifty. Academic adult English flipped completely. Forty-eight of the fifty most used words in college come from Latin.

The top fifty words in each category was a good start. But we are talking about 150 words. I was still skeptical. To really test this, along with one of my classes I put together 20,000 words learned at different ages. The finding was the same: for native English speakers, Germanic words dominated in childhood and Latin-based words dominated in adolescence. Native speakers are faster and more accurate when reading English words that come from German. The really interesting part was when we looked at nonnative English speakers. Of course, they were in general worse than native speakers. However, they showed the opposite pattern. Nonnative speakers were better at recognizing Latin-based words than Germanic ones.

When I talk to people about these data, they often remind me that vocabulary is not everything. I mean, if you say that English has a lot of Latin vocabulary, then you cannot claim that it is part German, part Latin. It just has a lot of vocabulary, but really it is still English, a Germanic language.

Actually, that is not entirely true either. Some of the words that came into English from Latin bring some of their grammar with them. For example, in English I can say something like, "Domino's gave me a pizza." But I cannot say, "Domino's delivered me a pizza." To use "deliver," I would say, "Domino's delivered a pizza to me." Yet verbs that come from German like "give" can take an indirect object in the middle, as in "gave me the pizza," or at the end, as in "gave the pizza to me." However, a lot of verbs in English that are derived from Latin can only be used grammatically in one way: "delivered the pizza to me." Thus, the origin of a verb plays a role in its grammatical usage.

We can stop for a second and think about it using the idea of infolding that was introduced earlier. The very basic early learned parts of English come from German. Native speakers will learn to use these pretty automatically. Think about the sentence "I gave it to him" versus "He gave it to me." "He" versus "him" and "I" versus "me" just sound right. The basics come to form the base of the language. This is much like learning to dribble the ball while learning to walk, as Byer found in soccer. Building these core skills comes first. Later comes the learning of more advanced skills such as passing, blocking, and strategy. In English, these advanced skills are based on Latin words.

Now we can turn back to what made Joseph Conrad such a great writer in English. He was lucky in multiple ways. He learned to write in a language that was highly simplified to accommodate late learners of a language. The second piece of luck was that he had learned French, a language that was close to English due to the Norman invasion that had occurred many centuries before he wrote his epic piece. Third, he had learned Latin and Greek. Let me show you the passage that Conrad wrote from this perspective. I have marked the origins of the words so that you can see this point more clearly. The Latin-based words are in italics and the German-based ones are underlined.

> The day was ending in a *serenity* of still and *exquisite brilliance*. The water shone *pacifically*; the sky, without a speck, was a *benign immensity* of unstained light; the very mist on the Essex marsh was like a *gauzy* and *radiant fabric*, hung from the wooded rises inland, and draping the low shores in *diaphanous* folds. Only the gloom to the west, brooding over the upper reaches, became more *sombre* every minute, as if angered by the *approach* of the sun.

Conrad was exploiting English by peppering in the elegance of French and Latin between a set of very basic German-like phrases. It is both simple and elegant. Now, imagine he had written it almost entirely in Latin-based English. Here is my attempt at that:

> The diurnal completion was embedded in a silent serenity and exquisite brilliance. The aqueous fluorescence floated pacifically; the atmosphere, vacant of fragments, was a benign immensity of pristine luminosity, the vapor floating on top of the Essex bayou was similar to the inferior front in diaphanous corrugates. The singular misery to the occident, menacing over the superior extents, transformed to an increased solemnity as the minutes passed, infuriated by the ascension of the solar mass.

Whoa! It is almost like a foreign language, something you would read in a biology or science text. Churchill might have declared the English language a means to spread Anglo influence in the world. The reality is that English is a modern creole, composed of a German core and a Latin wrapping. It is the quintessential emergent form, molded by its history to make it amenable to most of western Europe.

Conrad, as an educated Polish man, had multiple advantages when writing English. It's ironic that a nonnative speaker could be thought of as having advantages. Just one small reminder: it is a very specific type of nonnative speaker that has these advantages when writing academic English.

BEYOND CONRAD

In this chapter, we considered how children learn language through sound. Most hyperpolyglots seem to use a similar strategy. They take sound pieces and then add the ability to stand outside of language. This leaves the rest of us. If we are lucky, we will try our hand at English as a foreign language. Here individuals from western Europe have a particular advantage. A person can come in through Latin and learn a specialized form of academic English. He or she could also choose the simpler Germanic form of English. If this is the case, then a simplified grammar allows a nonnative speaker a way in to communicate the most basic needs. Both the adolescent-like and adultlike route to English work for different purposes.

What about all the other languages? What happens if you want to learn Mandarin, Russian, Arabic, or Japanese? I just took a deep breath because it is much harder for an English speaker. The same applies for people coming from non–western European backgrounds. English for a Mandarin speaker requires rote memorization, at least according to a graduate student from China who took my class. There is very little to hang on to. And, of course, you have so many other language combinations. We could think of a native speaker of Japanese trying to learn Russian or Mandarin, a native speaker of Quechua trying to learn Spanish, or a native speaker of Pashto learning Hindi. Learning a new language as an adult comes in many different flavors.

My advice would be to try and find the music in language. The rules are hard to learn. As adults, we will inevitably try to establish absolute certainty about when to use a grammatical form. Instruction helps and rules guide us. But if you can, try somehow to work on the core of language, the sounds and sound patterns. Try to see if you can learn to imitate the sounds someone makes in another language. It may seem trivial to just babble meaningless combinations. Reiterer's work suggests that learning a new language is related to learning its sound.

There is one final piece of advice that might help a person when learning a new language. Everyone has their own path. And this path often is not straight. As we will see next, Ash Barty found her own way to the top of women's tennis by taking a gap year. In her case, the gap year was more like a year and a half. Nonetheless, putting a pause on her tennis had remarkable effects on her ability to improve once she returned.

CASE STUDY: HOW CRICKET MADE ASH BARTY A BETTER TENNIS PLAYER

ASH BARTY'S INITIAL ASCENT

In 2019, I gave a couple of presentations on the bilingual brain. I personally had experienced in a very real way the physical nature of language learning. This happened when my northeastern accent came out one day when I was singing in Portuguese. I also experienced it when I went to Mexico at the age of fourteen. In these episodes, I saw that my language system seemed to shift. My interest had been captured by Ashleigh Barty, who had left tennis for almost two years before coming back to it. In a way, much of what Ash experienced fit in with my own language experience.

I was giving a talk in Montreal, Canada, and when I was preparing my talk she was ranked No. 11 in the world. By the time I gave my talk she was on her way to being ranked No. 9 after winning her semifinal match at the Miami Open.

Two months later, I would be in Pittsburgh giving a talk in honor of my colleague Brian MacWhinney. In this talk, I posited that the way Ash Barty used cricket to reshape her tennis had a lot of

Picture of Ash Barty's tennis forehand and of batting during a cricket game. *Wikimedia Commons.*

Wikimedia Commons.

similarities to the emergence of skill in language learning. I even included a picture in which I showed the transfer of these skills from one sport to the other.

Because her ranking was changing so quickly, I had to keep crossing out numbers on my slide.

During that particular talk, Ash happened to be playing the finals of Roland-Garros (the French Open). A proud Australian in the audience beamed as I talked about Ash and quickly looked up the score. She had won the first set and was up in the second set of the finals. She would go on to win the tournament and eventually take the No. 1 ranking. To me the interest in Ash went beyond just admiration for sport. To me it illustrated basic principles of development.

Ash Barty batting during a cricket game. *Getty images.*

ASCENT INTERRUPTED

Piaget's theory of cognitive development requires us to ask fundamental questions about the role of childhood in the development of a skill or ability. Rather than thinking about children as a builder collecting tools in a toolbox, Piagetians would ask a very different question. A neo-Piagetian, like me, would ask how a person grows across time and what skills should be put in place so that he or she can grow in a certain direction. As an emergentist, I think a lot about how things get put together and how they may fall apart. I think about a trajectory, a path along which each person travels in his or her ultimate attainment. One interesting aspect of trajectory is that we are often captivated by what appears to be a fast rise to the top.

I first stumbled across the idea of a trajectory in sports when I bought a book that would help me understand how my kids could learn to play tennis. The first thing that was made clear by the author was that as a coach we cannot expect our children to spontaneously become Martina Hingis. During her time, Hingis would become the poster child of a prodigy. Martina was named for Martina Navratilova by her mother, Melanie Moltorova, who had been a top player in Czechoslovakia. The name fit her perfectly: Hingis was a phenom. She learned to play tennis at age two and entered her first tournament at age four. By age twelve she was winning junior tournaments and became the junior French Open champion. A year later she won the junior French Open again and topped that with a Wimbledon junior championship. She became the youngest at the time to ever win a major championship when just a few months after her sixteenth birthday she won the Australian Open.

Ash Barty was an interesting deviation from the path taken by Martina Hingis. Like many pros, Barty began young, at the age of four. Her junior coach Jim Joyce was not really keen on working with very young children. Barty was different. She had excellent hand-eye coordination and could hit the ball back at a very young age. She used to practice against the outside wall of her house for hours on end. Within a few years she was beating children who were years older than her, and by age twelve she was playing with men.

From there her career met with continued success. She was a junior phenom, winning the Wimbledon junior championships and making the semifinals of the US Open Juniors at age fifteen. Two years later she made it to the finals of three major tournaments in doubles and achieved her highest ranking, No. 12 in doubles. However, her success in singles did not come as easily as her ranking was consistently outside the top 100. Ash was stuck and her scaling of the tennis rankings seemed to stall.

The pressure grew too great and at some point, Barty decided to take a break from tennis. Weeks turned into months. Ash never abandoned tennis entirely, though; she continued playing tennis while taking a break from competition.

A DETOUR

At one point, the coach of a local cricket club, the Brisbane Heat, invited her to meet with the players to talk about how it felt to be on the road. Ash had traveled a lot, but for the cricket players it was something new. The coach figured that Ash might be able to help them with this aspect of competition.

The chemistry was instant, and the team coach invited her to hit a few balls and see how she felt. Barty's hand-eye coordination and ability to learn quickly were apparent immediately. She could hit balls very well and her fielding was superb for someone who had just played informally. Barty reported feeling happy to spend time with the team, where everyone worked together to improve. The camaraderie and the chance to do something else were refreshing.

The change in her routine also had another effect, one that was predicted by Grosser and Schonborn in their review of junior tennis development. The authors proposed two different trajectories, one in which a child specializes early and learns to "trick" his or her way into winning many matches. I remember watching my son play tennis when he was twelve. At that point the kids were playing with regular balls. Most of the matches consisted of very slowly hit high balls. The way to win was to simply keep hitting high balls over and over again. The problem was that playing this way did not prepare my son for what was coming. Just a few years later at sixteen or eighteen, tennis looked entirely different. The balls were zooming by and the path the ball took was on a much flatter curve. The important thing in tennis was to develop the skills that would be needed later. This would involve learning to hit balls around waist height coming very quickly.

This is similar to the point made by Tom Byer when it came to learning to manipulate the ball. His view was that children were being moved into competition before they developed the basic skills on which they could build a more complete game. If they moved into competition too early, they might learn tricks to win. This could be something like using brute strength or speed, or relying on weak defenses that could defend only on one side. As competition improved, these tricks would stop working. For Byer, it was important to move the ball with both feet from the beginning. By developing these basic skills, a player would be ready for stiffer competition later.

Grosser and Schonborn suggest that early success can be counterproductive when it is not in line with the types of skills that are needed later. In many cases, many early champions begin to show a drop-off in their abilities after puberty and an eventual decline as they enter their twenties. Other children who work instead on their fundamental skills—much like Byer proposed in soccer—will surpass those who peak early and continue improving well into their twenties and begin showing a drop-off in their early thirties.

After completing one season with the Brisbane Heat, Barty returned to tennis. With a renewed focus and a fresh outlook, Barty picked up where she had left off, rising again in doubles and reaching a career high of No. 11 in the world in singles. While the stories of Ash Barty and Martina Hingis are intriguing from the prodigy perspective, they are also instructive from the perspective of the types of changes that occur during adolescence and their relationship to the two trajectories proposed by Grosser and Schonborn.

Martina peaked during this early period around age fifteen to eighteen and did very well up until the age of twenty-two. At twenty-two, she began a steep drop-off in ability as she struggled with injuries, and she eventually left professional tennis altogether. She returned to tennis after several operations on the tendons in her ankles. As was the case for other children pushed to the brink who eventually require surgery, her body was not able to tolerate the strain of professional tennis. Given the large number of child athletes who are entering operating rooms at earlier and earlier ages, we are left wondering if some of Hingis's injuries might have begun during her childhood and early adolescence as she ascended at such a fast pace. The graph of her ascendancy showing very early success and then a gradual decline in early adulthood is similar to those seen in Grosser and Schonborn's early peaking group.

Although Hingis made several comebacks in singles, she never reached the heights she had obtained as a teenager. Later in her "final" comeback, she continued to play doubles and became world No. 1 and won several major titles with a variety of partners. Unlike Hingis, Barty interrupted her tennis career at precisely the time that she was ascending. She picked up an entirely different game that uses a similar but different set of skills. Barty credits this period with her taking a break from the rigors of travel and an individual sport. It also brought her something else: it disrupted her tennis.

THE POWER OF DISRUPTION

Recent work in brain science shows that rather than being a time dedicated purely to specialization in very specific skills, adolescence is also a time of great change. Váša and colleagues, in order to understand neural changes during adolescence, looked at how brain areas communicate with each other in a group of fourteen- and twenty-six-year-olds by scanning them at six-month intervals. During their analyses they found two different types of cerebral cross talk. Areas that were devoted to motor and sensory process- ing—called *primary areas*—showed activity that was strong al- ready and grew even stronger over time. These areas are involved in actions like movements of body parts and processing of informa- tion from the senses. They are the areas responsible for the types of things that young children do. The fact that these sensorimotor areas remain strong in adolescence suggests that the basic circuits built up in childhood are still important in adolescence and receive further bolstering during this period.

While activity in the sensorimotor cortex was growing stronger, other areas of the brain were showing a disruptive pattern. Disrup- tion, in the authors' view, was due to two different and opposing forces. The brain activity between some areas grew weaker in those that had previously been strongly connected. At the same time, connections between areas that had been more weakly in- terconnected grew more strongly interconnected. It was as if the brain was retuning itself from a childlike form to an adultlike form of processing.

The interconnections that showed the greatest increase in strength were between association areas as well as connections between sub- cortical and cortical areas. Association areas are those that link infor- mation between different senses or between senses and motor areas. They are involved in what researchers call *higher-level cognition*, or what Piaget would term *formal operations*. This includes cognitive functions such as memory, understanding what others are thinking— called *theory of mind*—and the processing of language.

The other set of interconnections that grew stronger were those involved in cortical–subcortical communication. The cortex is the newest part of our brains and is involved in all the complex think- ing, moving, and sensing that we do. Subcortical areas are involved in basic sensing and moving. The communication between these areas is needed to help fine-tune our ability to keep multiple types of information in mind. These connections are needed when we have to adapt to new tasks or switch between two known tasks. The fact that association areas are crucial for problem-solving, flexibility, and the ability to delay gratification suggests that adolescence is a time of learning to better adapt to the outside world.

During her ascent to a higher spot in the tennis hierarchy, Ash Barty chose to embrace a very tumultuous time. In fact, she actually enhanced her tennis (and herself!) by yielding to the voices of disruption. Rather than just focusing on the hyperspecialization of the skills that were already in place, she sought to break them up and jiggle them around.

During my talk, many people in the audience began to wonder about my main point, that the lessons of disruption, flexibility, and adaptability that a brain learning multiple languages shows is similar to other motor skills. One person even asked whether there might be a problem with my analogy. People who learn a language later in life are not always as successful. They often have strong accents and smaller vocabularies and make grammatical mistakes.

My answer is that people who learn a second language later in life speak, read, and write differently. Similarly, Ash played with a different style compared to other players. Her tennis in a way absorbed parts of her cricket game. Rather than focusing on the differences we could focus on the similarities and the way in which skills learned for one language can transfer to another.

In sport, we can think of similar types of cross-training that have become part of the regimen of many athletes. In 2015, I began to develop very severe pain in my left leg. It made playing tennis painful and running—which had been my method of building aerobic fitness—impossible. I decided that I would go run in the shallow section of the pool at the University of Houston. At first this was just to build up my leg muscles without the pounding. Unable to play tennis or run, there were periods when I would go up to three times a week.

Eventually, the pain stopped, and I was able to run and play tennis again. The interesting thing was that I felt like I was running differently. In tennis, I felt that I could run forward faster and with better posture. Working against the water made my movement even better. I have done similar things with my daughter Kamille. For example, Milo, our dog, likes to run away from us. Part of her workout regimen is to have her chase Milo around and try to catch him. If you have seen *Rocky II*, you might remember a similar version of this in which Balboa, the left-handed "Italian Stallion," is told by his trainer to chase the chicken. This was designed to make him move his feet. I borrowed this idea and asked Kamille to catch Milo.

Sometimes I have her just kick a soccer ball around with her brother. We also do other exercises that are designed to help her tennis but also make sure she is in good shape. This can involve running or throwing medicine balls. I was even thinking of getting her a mitt and hitting her some softballs, just to get her used to catching balls and to get her off the court.

Like the researcher who questioned whether tennis and cricket for Barty were like learning another language, we can easily think about progress along only one dimension. How good are we at a very narrow skill? Emergentists ask different questions: What are the pieces that need to be put together along a path? How do those pieces rejiggle themselves? Can we actually do better by disrupting the process? How much can we actually leverage the incredible flexibility that we have as organic beings to do even better? Ash Barty in some ways showed me that the way forward is not always straight. Sometimes we need to take a turn or even several turns. And when we do, we end up moving forward more than we had ever imagined.

Having finished my talk, I was eager to know how Ash Barty, who had become an interesting analogy for the flexible and adaptive nature of (language) learning, had done in the finals of the French Open. I sat down opened my laptop and saw the pictures of her being crowned the French Open women's singles champion.

11

A GENE RARELY DOES ITS WORK ALONE

YOU CAN'T ALWAYS GET WHAT YOU WANT

The phrase made famous by the Rolling Stones was one that resonates quite clearly with one of my childhood dreams. Growing up in Oakland, California, I became absorbed by sports. Baseball was the one that I watched the most. Football was brought on by all my friends. But somewhere deep in my heart there was nothing more admirable than being a baller—a basketballer, that is.

My basketball *career* started in school during recess. A group of us not-so-athletic players would gather to play on one of the courts. When the lunch or recess bell rang, I could not wait to get out to the court and play. I became so bent on becoming better that I asked for a basketball hoop for my eleventh birthday. I helped my dad put it up in the backyard at my mom's house. There was no cement, so I would mostly practice shooting since dribbling was not very feasible.

Now I had recess, lunch, and after school to play. Whatever thing did not work on the playground I would bring home. My homework was to practice shooting for thirty to forty-five minutes every day. Since I was not the tallest player on the court, I had to learn to adapt. One shot I learned was the hook shot. You basically stand sideways and use your body to block the defender as you release the ball with the opposite hand. Kareem Abdul-Jabbar made the hook shot famous. From his height of seven feet, Abdul-Jabbar actually made a skyhook. It was basically untouchable by any player. I spent hours practicing my hook shot. I was not seven feet tall, but it served me well, nonetheless.

At fourteen, I was stuck well below six feet (1.83 meters), and I never got close enough to even dream of playing any kind of organized basketball beyond the junior high playground. I went into retirement at age twenty-six when in a pickup game I decided to guard a player who was much faster and more athletic than I was. As I raced to cover him, I landed on someone's foot, ended up in the emergency room with a basketball-sized ankle, and spent two weeks on crutches. It was six weeks before I could get back to tennis.

Even though I had unofficially "retired" from basketball, one day the sport just popped into the tennis court unannounced. That particular day, I was hitting overheads the way people normally hit them. The overhead is one of the most cherished and dreaded shots in tennis. In desperation, your opponent is feeling pressure. They are either pulled off the court and they need time to get back onto the court or they simply feel that if they hit you a lob you might miss. I once missed thirteen overheads in a row on a sunny day against my very good friend Reza. He had incredible feel and he could seemingly lob from anywhere on his side of the net to anyplace on my side. Anyone who has played tennis has watched an overhead smash miss its mark. Even professional tennis players who have the best overheads will occasionally miss one. It comes with the game.

Like everyone else who plays tennis, I was practicing my overhead in order to avoid the calamity of missing this shot. There are some lobs, however, that are not hit with the intent of being high but are actually hit quickly over your head. Because the ball is falling quickly, a regular overhead often misses because the tennis racket is either pointing up and the ball goes long or it is pointing down and the ball hits the net. But on one particular day, out of the blue I got a short lob and my skyhook just appeared out of nowhere.

Tennis players call this a *bolo shot*. Rather than hitting above, the player lets the ball go over the head and then jumps to catch it with his or her racket. It is like a hook shot with a racket in one's hand. Since I am catching the ball behind me, I am able to control the lower ball and put it in the court. It is one of my favorite shots. When I hit it, people look at me like I have done something they have never seen before. A pro once told me that I should just hit every overhead that way. If you watch old replays of Jimmy Connors, you will see what I mean. He used this bolo overhead a lot of the time.

I never got to do what I dreamed of. The slam dunk and the hook shot never made it past the playground. But the bolo overhead has hung around like a vestigial remnant from my childhood. I am essentially compensating for my lack of height by hitting the ball up from behind rather than hitting it in front of me.

Whatever constraints Mother Nature laid on my height, I more than made up for them with adaptability. My dad was five feet ten (178 cm) and my mom was five feet (152.4 cm). At five feet seven (165.1 cm) I have been told by those much taller than me that I have one of the best overheads they have ever seen. That from a former college player. And so my dream of playing basketball got grafted into the game of tennis I play today. Rather than letting any genetic limitation get in my way, I found a way around it so that I could continue doing my homework in a different sport.

NATURE, NURTURE, OR NONE OF THE ABOVE

Height is something that is genetically determined. Most of it is driven by our parents. Sometimes these genes don't work as advertised and individuals can be much taller or shorter than their parents. But in general, height can be predicted pretty accurately with a simple family history. One question that arises is how far our genetic heritage takes us. What happens when we move beyond height to other arenas, such as learning motor skills, languages, or games?

The way in which our genetic predisposition does or does not shape the eventual outcome in whatever endeavor we undertake is the topic of considerable discussion. Robert Plomin has dedicated his career to trying to understand the extent to which genes and environment contribute to an individual's ability. In his book *Blueprint*, Plomin openly states that environments are extremely variable. They change so much that they cannot be the principal driving force in making us different. In Plomin's view, the only constant in our lives are the genes we are born with. According to Plomin, these serve as a type of compass or a scaffold that leads us to our true selves. Even the greatest proponent of practice as the best route to improvement had to make some concessions to genetics. The most obvious genetic trait is height. I suppose my parents knew that I had a very slim chance of ever reaching a height close to that of a pro basketball player. No matter what my parents or I did, my genetic destiny would take me off the basketball court for good. In a similar vein, weight is driven in great part by our genes. Some people simply have more of a tendency to gain weight than others. All things being equal, there are those who can eat seemingly whatever they want and never gain weight. There are others who have to keep their guard up. In my case, it's a bit of both.

One question I have always asked myself is what would happen if we brought two people together with opposite views. What would happen if Plomin and Ericsson had a conversation? Plomin represents the idea that genetics is the guiding force. Environments are too variable to matter. Ericsson states that genetics matters only for physical attributes. In Ericsson's view, deliberate practice is the main driving force. We can all change the way we practice. We can all excel. It has to do with practice, and that can be bolstered via the environment. The Plomin versus Ericsson debate leaves us wondering how two very influential researchers can come to such different conclusions.

Debates between nature and nurture are ones that have moved from the realm of philosophy to psychology. Psychology presents us with three different ways that we can resolve the nature versus nurture debate. We can come out on one side in the way that Ericsson or Plomin did, or we can come out somewhere in between. It's the in-between posture that is harder to make sense of. More recently, Kathryn Paige Harden, in her book *The Genetic Lottery*, makes the case that genes should be considered when thinking about educational outcomes. Heredity is just as strong as socioeconomic status when considering how long someone stays in school. If genes are that powerful, shouldn't we put them into our research and work on how to improve college completion rates? Harden is championing an in-between approach in which the environment— that is, our socioeconomic status—and the genes we inherit from our parents both contribute to educational outcomes.

So we can start by arguing that both matter. This still leaves us with a question: how is it that both the genes and the environment matter? Let's start this by considering genetics with regard to language.

LANGUAGE ACQUISITION AND THE GRAMMAR GENE

At the end of the twentieth century, a battle over the soul of our cognitive abilities erupted. One camp argued very strongly that our ability to learn language was driven by an innate capacity for language. This genetic predisposition to language had gained such support that it made it to the *NBC Nightly News*, where Tom Brokaw declared that researchers had discovered "the gene for grammar."

The idea that language is part of an innate language acquisition device was brought to prominence by Noam Chomsky. In a nutshell, Chomsky saw a very complicated language system, a baby born with very little language, and a sudden appearance of a very complex system at a young age. The grammar gene idea came about due to a freak discovery by a group of researchers headed by Myrna Gopnik, a famous Canadian developmental psychologist. Fate would have it that I would meet many of her students by chance at a conference that neither of us normally attended.

One day, Liz Bates showed up at my office in the laboratory, where I was busy working on some data analysis. She sat down and told me that there was a conference on aphasia, a language disorder due to stroke, that was taking place outside Montreal. It was two weeks long so there was no way she could go. She hated the idea of missing it. So she wanted to know if she could send me, as long as I promised to take a lot of notes. Hmmm . . . travel to Canada for the first time, stay at a conference, and meet all these important researchers. All of this in exchange for notes. I liked the deal and took it on the spot. Of course, the biggest bonus was that your adviser had thought of you and not someone else to fill her shoes.

Liz was sending me much farther north and east than I had ever traveled. Up until that point, my travel map was a strange one. On the northern end was Reno, Nevada; the southwestern corner was just south of Santiago, Chile; and the southeast was in Argentina. The farthest east I had traveled in the United States was Austin, Texas. Montreal was not on that map. The two-week retreat was not even in Montreal per se. When I got off the plane, I headed to a bus that would take us on the hour-long ride outside the city. There I arrived at a house in the woods where researchers would gather to talk about their studies and work on the new edition of a book.

To say this house was secluded is an understatement. This was 1994, so the world was just barely starting its wireless transcontinental connecting project. There was one wired phone for the entire house. There was no TV and there was no Internet connection. I could not even check email or find out what was going on in the world very easily.

Because the meeting venue was isolated and there was no TV and no Internet, the time off was spent speaking to other people. At one gathering, I met a group of students from Canada. As we spoke, the students were surprised that I was getting along so well with them. Out of the blue one of the students asked me, "Did you know that our advisers hate each other?" I had no idea of this conflict. The reason for the strong disagreement would appear a little later in my trip.

I had heard my doctoral adviser complain bitterly about a new book by Steven Pinker called *The Language Instinct*. When I spotted one of the friendly students from the "enemy" camp reading it, I asked her what she thought about it. She told me it was a great book and that it featured the research by her adviser about a special family in England. According to the student, this family was perfectly normal. They were doctors, lawyers, and held other professional jobs. The only problem with them was that they could not produce the regular past tense. Instead of saying something like "I **walked** to the store yesterday," they would say, "I **walk** to the store yesterday." They could not add an -*ed* to the end of a verb to change it from the present to the past tense.

This finding led researchers to conclude that the family had difficulty with grammatical rules. The KE family does exist, and they do have an impairment that results in a deficit that can be seen in the way they use language. Their impairment is called *autosomal dominant*. I put in a family tree below so that you can see it better.

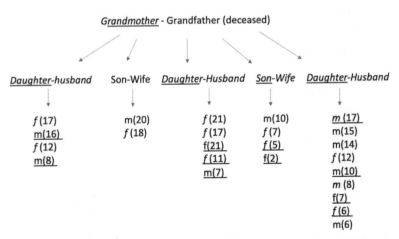

Diagram of the autosomal dominant disorder seen in the *KE family. Underlines indicate affected member. Adapted from Gopnik and Crago (1991).*

When I heard about this family and about the money that was coming in to study the genetics behind their grammar problems, I began to wonder if there might actually be a grammar gene. Maybe there was an innate genetically determined scaffold that all humans use to learn grammar. The graduate students seemed very pleasant, and we were able to socialize without any conflicts. They admired their mentor just as much as I admired mine.

This very classic view of language development as arising from genetically led learning was contrary to what I had experienced. I had been exposed to multiple languages as a child: Spanish and English from birth. Farsi for a year in home care. If learning language was just me digging out grammatical rules that were buried in my genes, how was it that I managed to learn and forget Farsi in a year? What about the fact that I had sung in Brazilian Portuguese as a child, and that eventually led me to native-like ability in that language? How could a perfectly elaborated plan be given to me genetically to handle such an imperfect set of language experiences? Never mind that my adviser had said that language was "a new machine built out of old parts." Basically, she held that language emerged from a lot of different systems that worked together to help us communicate with others.

Outside Montreal with all the views that had been baked into my thinking called into question, I was left with one basic question that would determine whether I had been brainwashed or seen the light. "Have you ever met any of these family members?" I asked a student. "No, but I have read all about them," the student answered.

Seeing is believing, and if she had not seen them in person, there was enough doubt in my mind to suspend judgment until further information was available. My adviser might be wrong, but the word of a graduate student who was reporting things secondhand was not enough to convince me entirely. I had not seen this family myself, and that made me doubt whether it was all true. What I *did* know was what I had experienced as a child, and this did not fit in with a fixed set of grammar rules that are preprogrammed from birth. To me language was a lot more flexible than an instinct.

WHAT DOES THE "GRAMMAR" GENE REALLY DO?

The grammar gene that Myra Gopnik and her colleagues were taking about was one that codes for the protein forkhead box P2, shortened to FOXP2. It is a transcription factor, which means that it helps to regulate a lot of other genes. Most revealing is the role it plays, which the National Library of Medicine website (https://ghr .nlm.nih.gov/gene/FOXP2#conditions) describes as follows:

> Studies suggest that it plays important roles in brain development, including the growth of nerve cells (neurons) and the transmission of signals between them. It is also involved in synaptic plasticity, which is the ability of connections between neurons (synapses) to change and adapt to experience over time. Synaptic plasticity is necessary for learning and memory.
>
> The forkhead box P2 protein appears to be essential for the normal development of speech and language. Researchers are working to identify the genes regulated by forkhead box P2 that are critical for learning these skills.

Studies in language have found this gene to be linked to a disorder called *developmental dysphasia*. *Dysphasia* comes from the Greek *dusphatos*, which can be broken up into "difficulty" (*dus*) and "spoken" (*phatos*). Notice, however, that as a transcription factor, the FOXP2 gene works together with several other genes. FOXP2 fits in with the so-called one gene for one disorder (OGOD) approach. The idea behind this approach is that a single gene can be associated with a very specific malady. The effect of a single gene does appear in humans such as in sickle cell anemia. In this case, one gene regulates the form of hemoglobin. Two copies of a recessive gene lead to a maladaptive form of hemoglobin. One copy leads to resistance to malaria.

The work of Robert Plomin and colleagues takes a different approach to the single gene approach used for FOXP2 and the KE family. Rather than arguing that each gene codes for a single trait—along the lines of traditional views of Mendelian inheritance—they argue for quantitative trait loci (QTL). QTLs are collections of genes that together help to code for a trait. We can think of this as a type of distributed representation, which fits in with the notion of an emergent function. Let me give you a more concrete example to make the point.

One way to describe a distributed representation is to think about the joints needed to produce a tennis stroke. We would all agree that the wrist is crucial for tennis. Commentators on television often talk about the way that Roger Federer "hits his backhand with a flick of the wrist." However, the flick of the wrist is just the finish. It is actually the result of a lot of other little things. The stroke that ends with the wrist starts from his feet. This then travels like a wave up his legs, through his torso, shoulder, arm, and then culminates in his hand. We could think of this backhand as a skill that is distributed across his body and requires a coordination of multiple body parts across time. If you think about it that way, we also agree that all knowledge of tennis is *not* contained in our wrists. The wrist is just what we see at the end of what biomechanics experts call the *kinetic chain*, the progression of forces that go from one body part to the other.

Thinking about how all the different body parts coordinate to hit a tennis ball is analogous to how genes work. Researchers have found that most traits in humans are polygenic and can be linked to several genes. In other words, most traits (eye color, height, hand and finger size, etc.) are the product of many genes. For some of the more complex traits such as those measured by psychologists, the number of genes is quite high and the ability to figure out how they are inherited becomes much more difficult because the effects of any single gene is very weak.

To add even more complexity to the picture, the environment can actually serve as a trigger that causes genes to be expressed or not. Recent research points to a complex but intriguing interplay between the genes we inherit from our parents and the environments that can trigger them. The effects of the environment as triggers have been traced to what geneticists call *epigenetics*. The notion of epigenetics is not a new one. It came about many years ago when Conrad Waddington proposed that development occurs across a type of landscape that can take us in very different directions.

WADDINGTON AND THE EPIGENETIC LANDSCAPE

Conrad Waddington is known for popularizing the notion that environments interact with genes. However, he was not the first one to propose that our experiences could modify our inheritance of traits. In 1797, Lamarck had proposed that evolution involved passing changes that occurred in one generation on to the next generation. As time went by each generation would experience a certain environment that was then passed on to the next generation, and so on and so forth. Lamarck's ideas would make it into Darwin's theory published in 1859. However, many scientists later came to see Lamarck's ideas as unduly simplistic. For example, in 1889 August Weismann tested whether it was possible to change the physiology of an organism by doing something to its ancestors. Weismann cut off the tails of mice for five successive generations. However, he was never able to get rid of a mouse's tail. All the pups were born with tails.

Because of this resistance to environmental manipulations, Weismann argued that there is a barrier between inherited traits and what happens in a person's lifetime. In other words, what happens to us today will not affect how our children will develop. Weismann was arguing that the environment could not make a trait go away. This also meant that if a parent grew larger muscles

with exercise, this could not be passed down to the next generation. Based on these studies with mice, Weismann concluded that
whatever happened in an animal's lifetime could not affect subse-
quent generations.

The idea of a fixed genetic inheritance changed when Waddington began to think more deeply about Weismann's experiment.
He noted that cells start out with very little specialization during
early fetal development. Cells become specialized by moving to
a particular cellular environment. Waddington took this idea and
expanded it to human traits. Rather than thinking of development
as eliminating a given trait, he began to consider how the environment causes traits to vary in one direction or the other. His main
idea was that even people with identical genetic makeups could
have different phenotypes. Heredity was not destiny.

An example of epigenetic changes can be seen when dietary
changes affect an entire population. My dad observed this first-
hand as a teenager in Japan when my grandfather was sent to
work there for UNESCO. One of the images that most stood out
in his mind was seeing Japanese teenagers who towered over their
parents. Changes in nutrition had a major impact on Japanese
children. This change was much too fast for it to involve genetics.
The difference in height between parents and their children is the
range of variation in Waddington's view. The change in nutrition is
the environment that takes an individual along a path toward one
height or the other.

Thus, the environment can change the height of an individual,
increasing and decreasing it. In the case of Japan, height increases
were registered between 1950 and 2010. These changes are due
to a number of environmental variables, including increases in the
consumption of dairy-based protein (e.g., milk). Increases in GDP
also led to an increase in leisure time that can be devoted to sports.
This can stimulate growth of bones, especially in the legs. This has
led to an increase in height of about three to four inches (eight to
ten centimeters).

The increase in height across an entire generation is interesting in light of Waddington's epigenetic landscape. In fact, it suggests that environments do matter even for height, which has one of the strongest relationships across generations. The interesting thing is that this trend has not reversed itself. That is, Japanese children did not go back to being the height of their ancestors. This environmental effect might seem like an interesting exception to the genetic rule proposed by Plomin. Alternatively, it might be that we need to rethink what an environment might mean. To do this, we can turn to the work of another emergentist, Mark Johnson, who proposes that we rethink what nature and nurture are.

ENVIRONMENTS, BLUEPRINTS, AND THE BAUPLAN

In early circles of developmental biology, researchers often referred to a *bauplan*, or blueprint. The compound German word is a combination of *bau*, which means "build," and "plan," which is a cognate. So the German word gives us a slightly different meaning in that a "build plan" sounds a bit more elaborate than a blueprint, which we often equate with a sketch. A *bauplan* gives the feeling of an algorithm or a program that sets up what happens when.

When we dig deeper into neurobiology we find that it becomes harder to think about environments. Let's take the height analogy a bit further. In the case of Japan in the late twentieth century, height increased on average by a few inches. This was due to the fact that the environment changed, leading to an increased leg length. According to some researchers, we can use this as an analogy for all development. A baby is exposed to one environment after birth, a different one before birth, and so on and so forth. Very early in development, cells are very flexible. These stem cells can turn into any kind of cell depending on the cellular environment.

We can think of this as an extension of Teilhard de Chardin's infolding principle. Basically, at each stage of development environments vary. Cells have their own environment early on. They become more specialized across development and start to form clusters that become organs, hands, feet, and brains. These fold in on themselves as we get older and older. Each new form has its own environment at each level.

From this perspective we can actually flip Plomin's view on its head. Yes, the environment varies greatly. However, that does not make it less relevant. Rather, it makes it more important than ever when we consider that environments should vary. And they should vary *a lot*. Across ages we have different needs. Those needs are served by the outside world in different ways. It is a pretty amazing biochemical dance that leads us down the epigenetic landscape that Waddington imagined.

I realize at this point you might be wondering if we can move beyond cells, genes, and blueprints. I tried my best to explain this with nutrition and height. But let's try one more analogy to see if we can see epigenetics at work. Let's think about the Achilles tendon as the physical, genetically determined trait, and the environment as the amount of training needed to make it viable as the instrument for a world-class high jumper.

THE SPACE BETWEEN PRACTICE AND PERFECT

In his book titled *The Sports Gene*, David Epstein discusses the nature/nurture debate in the context of athletic endeavors. One of my favorite examples from that book is that of Stefan Holm, a Swedish high jumper who won the Olympic gold medal with a dogged training style. Holm was a young soccer player who became inspired by Patrik Sjöberg, a famous high jumper. At the young age of eight, Holm began to pursue his dream of being an Olympic high jumper. The problem was that Holm was not particularly tall. To address his height limitations he found a way to use his speed to help propel himself over the bar. Epstein details the ups and downs (pun intended) of his progress. Holm did not have immediate success and although he was very good it was not clear that he would win at the highest levels. However, every step back resulted in two steps forward. When it appeared that he had stalled at his highest level, Holm began an intense leg strengthening regimen on his left side. This turned his Achilles tendon into what Epstein calls "an unusually powerful launching mechanism." Holm attributes all his prowess to training. He even points to a Swedish translation of the book *Outliers*, noting that it was the ten thousand hours that had led him to beat many of the same people who had beaten him as a child. In this view, extreme practice led to Holm's talent. He had basically taken his Achilles tendon and made it into his weapon in his war on height.

Epstein continues by detailing a very different story. A few years after Holm won his Olympic gold, the world of high jump was changed by the arrival of a new competitor. Unlike Holm, Donald Thomas had not really even entertained the idea of becoming a high jumper. Thomas came to prominence at Lindenwood University, which is located in St. Charles, Missouri, a suburb northwest of St. Louis. Thomas had never trained for the high jump in his life. His entry into this new athletic endeavor came because of a challenge that he took on.

When Thomas bragged about being able to slam dunk, a few members of the track-and-field team challenged him to a high jump. Thomas had never really worn the right shoes and had no idea how to jump. Nevertheless, he cleared seven feet within a few attempts. Two months later he placed second at the National Association of Intercollegiate Athletics competition. His cousin Henry Rolle, the coach at Auburn, convinced Thomas to enroll and train for the high jump. With some additional coaching, Thomas was able to improve his form and use the right shoes to keep improving. By the time he met Holm at the 2007 world championships in Osaka, Japan, Thomas had been jumping only for a little over a year. Holm was the favorite but Thomas ended up beating him by getting close to eight feet off the ground with bad form and only seven months of training.

Many people marveled at Thomas's achievement. Several high jumpers had spent years training for the event. Holm lived in the alternative universe of athletic achievement where deliberate practice was the determining factor. He had essentially built one of the world's strongest Achilles tendons, whose purpose was to elevate him above the highest bars and into Olympic history. Thomas had been anything but deliberate. Yet his Achilles tendons were like springs, built up over time by his penchant for basketball and a long set of events on an evolutionary scale that had led to the development of a spring in his Achilles that was born out of a Darwinian clock that ticks not by the minute, the hour, or the year but by millennia. The 10,000 hours add up, but not everyone has the same starting point, and given the right combination of biological lottery and the appropriate environment in which to build up these skills, the clock can be accelerated, at least for the high jump.

If we think about Waddington's epigenetic landscape, we get a good understanding of how practice affects a person's genetic predisposition. In the case of Holm's achievement, we can see that he used extensive strengthening to create an Achilles tendon that allowed him to jump. Thomas, on the other hand, was on the extreme of natural physical variation. He had jumped quite a bit when playing basketball and in other venues. However, his tendon was due to heredity built to achieve height. Both athletes were exposed to an environment that took them to very similar outcomes. One required years of specialized training. The other required general training and reached greater heights. Within an epigenetic landscape, each represented a different path within his own personal range of ability.

When thinking about the role of practice in ultimate achievement, some research has begun to weigh in on the 10,000-hour deliberate practice view. In 2014, Brooke Macnamara, David Hambrick, and Frederick Oswald conducted a meta-analysis to look at this question. Meta-analyses are done taking into account many different studies to figure out how big an effect is. The idea is that each study might have slight flaws in its findings. However, if we take them all together then we can get a better picture of reality. Let's do a thought experiment here. Imagine a person who eats butter and bacon every day. The person goes on to live to the age of one hundred. Based on this one person, we might be led to think that bacon and butter are good for longevity. You test this on a group of people and then find the same thing in a particular region of the world. Voilà! The fountain of youth appears. The problem is that this might not hold true across regions and across different people. As studies continue on the butter and bacon (BB) longevity project, studies begin to find the opposite effects. Two different factions form, the pro-BB and the anti-BB. Then a debate ensues and researchers at a medical conference start dropping f-bombs on each other (no joke, this does happen sometimes).

One way to resolve this is to run a meta-analysis. Let's put all the studies together and see what happens. In many circles, the effects seen in my thought experiment are part of a larger dilemma in science: the need to make sure that our findings replicate. Let's take my BB analogy and apply it to sports. Consider McLaughlin (and his Dan Plan), Holm, and Thomas as examples. Each one of them represents an example of a point I am trying to make. McLaughlin and Holm represent the nurture side of an argument. McLaughlin had the idea that 10,000 hours would get him to a certain level of golf performance. Holm trained himself so hard in order to build an Achilles tendon that, paired with the momentum he built from running, would elevate him to a gold medal. Thomas is the counterexample. He represents a person who seems to have been endowed with an Achilles tendon that can elevate him to the highest levels of world competition. The problem with choosing examples to support a point is that we can always find counter-examples. What researchers would like to do is aggregate data, meaning to lump it together. A meta-analysis in which data from many different participants is brought together is one way to better understand the effects of practice on ultimate achievement.

Looking at ultimate achievement, Macnamara, Hambrick, and Oswald compiled a large number of studies on practice to see what effects they would have on ultimate attainment. If we take a lot of Stefan Holms and we look at them across a variety of fields, would his assertion that it was all practice hold up? The studies included four main areas of performance: games, music, sports, and education. The researchers also looked at other factors that might contribute to how well people performed. This included whether the particular area was predictable or not.

Examples we have considered vary along the predictability dimension. The order would be high jump (predictable), golf (somewhat predictable) and physics PhD (unpredictable). They found that the amount of deliberate practice depended on the particular area. It was substantial for games (26 percent), music (21 percent), and sports (18 percent) but not nearly as important in education (4 percent). Interestingly, education was the lowest and suggested that it might not be as predictable as other areas. Finally, the results held up regardless of method of collection. Taken together these results suggest that practice is very important. However, other factors also play a role in how well people perform in a domain.

One reading of this literature is that more practice does not lead to absolute better achievement. No matter how much Holm trained he would never jump as high as Thomas. What is lost in this discussion is that Holm could even jump as high as he did. The fact that he achieved world-class heights shows that there is more than one way to skin a cat. In other words, as humans we are able to excel using very different paths. While it is only a single number, the particular height a person reaches is a simple metric used to evaluate Thomas and Holm, and it does not capture the complexity of the ways in which these numbers were achieved. The process of jumping at world-class levels cannot be captured by a single number, just as the fact that I never hit a skyhook in official basketball competition should not be taken as a failure. It simply became a tool for a completely different venue. In my case, I used the skyhook to deal with balls that taller players hit with an overhead smash. In other words, at a lower height I adapted whatever I had to achieve the same outcome.

There is one last thing to consider here. Notice that practice seems to have a very small effect on education. Earlier I discussed the book by Kathy Paige Harden, *The Genetic Lottery*, in which she argues that heredity has an effect on education. I also discussed the KE family, who were missing a gene that is involved in the motor programs needed to speak. One interesting thing about education is that the effects appear to be as strong as those seen for physical attributes. One thing we might consider is that cognitive or mental tasks—like staying in school for many years or speaking to others—have a strong physical component. To stay in school, we need to sit for many hours at a time over multiple years. We need to read books and practice math equations, and we need to do these tasks over and over again. And then somehow we have to gain satisfaction from them. To speak well we need to hear the sounds that language makes and then repeat them. We need to internalize the sound combinations that form the base of grammatical rules. Everything mental is rooted in something physical.

The fact that genes and environments interact brings us to the ultimate test of the epigenetic landscape, the case of identical twins. As it turns out, "identical" is a misnomer because even though they are genetically identical, these twins are not identical. Even for those with the same genes, the environment can sway them in different directions.

12

CASE STUDY: SHUANGJIE AND ESTHER AND BOB AND MIKE

Identical Is Never Identical

THREE PERFECT STRANGERS

Our fascination with twins is easy to understand. Stories of nature and nurture gaining the upper hand can be found in the media. This includes TV, movies, and newspapers.

One example of this is in the film titled *Three Perfect Strangers* that documents the lives of a set of triplets who were separated and placed into three different homes. Each of these homes was in a different socioeconomic stratum: one lower, the second middle, and the third upper. The idea was that these three identical triplets would grow up in very different homes and hence the effect of genetics and the environment could be assessed. It was an illegal experiment performed without the knowledge of the birth parents, the adoptive parents, or the triplets.

The experiment was proceeding as it had originally been ill intentioned. All three triplets grew up separately. A person would go to gather data from all three families. However, it all came crashing down when the triplets met.

Their meeting was purely coincidental. One of them was attending a new college and to his surprise was treated as if everyone knew him. He then realized that there was another person who looked just like him, so two of the triplets ended up meeting in college. They found out about the third triplet through a friend. The similarities were so stark that all three were taken aback when they saw they were mirror images of each other.

At first, they seemed to be similar in many ways. They liked the same brand of cigarettes and similar types of women. All three wrestled in high school. After they met, they became a sensation on television and in the media. A lot was made of their similarities. The three of them opened a restaurant and became celebrities.

As the film continues, their differences become more and more apparent. One of the triplets suffered from bouts of depression. He eventually committed suicide. The film ponders the effect of environment. If they are all identical, why does only one of them commit suicide? This leads the other two to think about how each of their upbringings might have left one of them more vulnerable than the other.

The questions posed by this movie about the influence of genetics and the environment are ones that keep us up at night. Twins look identical to the naked eye, they, behave very similarly, and often they share the same preferences. Because identical twins seemed indistinguishable many considered them to be exactly the same. However, more recently scientists have uncovered interesting differences even in identical twins.

The story of the triplets serves as a backdrop for the current case study. Here we consider two opposite sets of twins. Mike and Bob Bryan, who grew up together and became a doubles tennis team, represent one end of the spectrum. On the other end are Esther and Shuangjie, two twins who were separated at birth and grew up in two different countries. Looking at both their stories offers us a glimpse into the ways in which genetics predisposes and the environment redisposes.

TWO PERFECT STRANGERS

An example of twins who grew up in very different environments is a pair born in China but separated at birth. In 2009, Barbara Demick reported on a young girl in the Hunan province of China who asked about her twin sister, who must be in the United States. The twins had been separated when they were a year old, when their mother had left one of the twins at her brother's house because she was having a hard time taking care of them. In May 2002, officials from a family planning office went and took the other twin away. She was taken to an orphanage. The family tried to get her back, but they were unsuccessful.

Demick, a reporter for the *Los Angeles Times*, promised Yuan, the twins' mother, that she would find her lost daughter. Demick tried to pursue some leads. She found a chat group on Yahoo that consisted of families who had adopted from the orphanage where Yuan's daughter had been placed. Demick found pictures of the children and shared them with her. Yuan identified her lost daughter. However, at the time the family in the United States was not willing to allow contact between their adopted daughter and her twin in China.

One morning ten years later, Demick got an email out of the blue letting her know that a family had an adopted daughter who they thought might have a twin sister in China. She answered the email and was able to arrange a reunion between the two. Demick proceeded slowly and deliberately. She had to consider the ethics and finally was able to work out an appropriate arrangement whereby she would translate letters that each twin wrote for the other.

The two girls wrote about what their lives were like. Shuangjie, in China, wrote about her interests in music, sports, and Chinese calligraphy. Esther had different interests that included art, photography, baking, and fashion. Esther had an American attitude based on self-achievement. She was already becoming a successful photographer. Shuangjie was more timid and less confident. Even though she was a very good student, she did not score high enough on the college entrance exams. Unable to attend college, she became a kindergarten teacher.

When the two girls met on video chat, they looked at each other for a long time. They looked identical, and genetics pretty much suggest with 100 percent probability that they are. However, Shuangjie was two inches taller, due at least partly to the fact that she had spent all her time at home whereas Esther had spent several months in an orphanage. In this most extreme of "natural" experiments, we can see that environments matter. Circumstances can take two twins who are as close as possible to genetically identical and lead them down very different paths, resulting in differences in educational attainment, hobbies, and interests. Growing up in completely different contexts does matter. It is fundamental to who we are as people.

It's Never Identical No Matter How Similar People Are

Shuangjie and Esther stand in stark contrast to Bob and Mike Bryan. The Bryan brothers are one of the most successful tennis double teams of all time. They have won 119 titles. They have won sixteen major tournaments, including winning Wimbledon three times. They have also won several Olympic medals, including the gold in 2012. They retired in 2020 after the coronavirus pandemic cut off what would be their final season.

The Bryan brothers seemed destined to become tennis legends from the moment they were born. Their mother Kathy excelled at tennis, winning the sixteen-and-under national championships in 1962. Later as a professional she reached No. 11 in the world in singles and No. 2 in doubles. She also made it to the semifinals in mixed doubles at Wimbledon and in women's doubles at the US Open. In singles she is in the *Guinness Book of World Records* for the longest match ever played, which is likely to stand since the rules have been changed to reduce match length. Wayne, their father, also played tennis, albeit with a lot less success than his wife, having competed in college tennis at University of California, Santa Barbara, and for a very short period on the pro tour in the early 1970s.

With an interest in tennis set in their heart, Wayne and Kathy set up the Cabrillo Racquet Club just north of Los Angeles. Both parents were eager for their twin sons to play tennis. Mike and Bob won their first tournament at the age of six. The Bryans not only played tennis together but also spent their entire tennis-playing lives together. They were so close to each other that they could count the number of times they had been apart. Most of those separations were marked by incessant and unending phone calls. When they went to college and were assigned different dorm rooms, Bob took his mattress to Mike's room and slept on the floor. Other teams saw them and thought they were telepathic. They rarely talked about strategy, seemingly moving in sync. Each knew what the other was going to do, something that most double teams struggle to do.

Even though they are identical twins, they are not identical. Bob is six feet four inches tall (193 centimeters). Mike is close to an inch (2 centimeters to be exact) shorter and weighs less. Bob is left-handed and Mike is right-handed. Both play with a one-handed backhand, but their styles differ slightly.

If tennis ability could be measured with a test, we would say that their performance is almost identical. Yet the way that they get there is not. The particular combination of tools they use and how they are combined are not the same. Bob has a bigger serve and a bigger, more explosive game. Mike hits his service returns more consistently and his volleys are very reliable. So their physical differences in height, weight, and handedness translate into different styles of play.

The three stories here about identical twins and triplets are only three stories. There are many more. These stories do, however, illustrate that development is a dance between the environment and an individual. Both matter, and to consider one as primary might make sense from a scientific point of view. As scientists we can focus on just one factor or we can use formulas to extract how much one counts compared to the other. Ericsson might have thought that each of these twin stories illustrated the importance of practice. If we write Chinese, we have to put in the hours to learn to make the characters. If we are going to be photographers, hours shooting photographs and then getting advice about how to improve matters. Tennis players need to practice in order to become professionals.

In the end, even if the scores are the same, the way two people get there—even if they are apparently identical—may not be so. People can write differently or may use slightly different strategies in any particular task. And therein lies the beauty of being human. The fact that we have an incredible amount of flexibility, that we adapt, is our gift. Even though the result might be the same, the way in which we put things together to create a result emerges out of the combination of lots of little things that don't really add up. Rather, they mix and meld to help us achieve something. The resulting combination is at the heart of our own individual roads to mastery.

13

OUR TWO SELVES

FROM ONE SELF TO THE OTHER

There is no substitute for practice. The Bryan brothers spent hours training for tennis. Dan spent hours perfecting his swing. Steve Falloon spent hours working on digit sequences. One of Anders Ericsson's first studies looked at how hours of deliberate practice differed between elite, near elite, and less skilled musicians. Polyglots, as studied by Maria Reiterer, were motivated to learn languages beyond those present in their immediate environment.

During these hours, those who practice might work on very minor things. It could be how to move your wrist or what type of image to hold in mind with each digit. Musicians might spend time working on a particularly difficult sequence. I would also spend a lot of time in my car driving around while repeating German phrases aloud that were played on CDs I had bought. The Bryan brothers would warm up for their matches by trading lightning-speed shots at each other at very close proximity.

A few years ago, after practicing a lot of tennis I began to notice something very peculiar. I could not form a mental image for myself as I performed the most essential task in tennis, hitting the ball. No matter how hard I concentrate, I cannot consciously see it. I lose the ball right before it hits my strings. And yet I am able to hit it just fine.

I can plan to hit the ball. I can move my feet to get in position. I can decide I want to practice this over and over again. This is my telling self that is acting. However, I cannot consciously control the actual moment right before contact. The ball just disappears from my conscious awareness.

All this talk about these two selves may seem strange. However, when we think about how our brain works, we are left with a lot of questions. If we cannot control our actions, how can we learn to improve? In particular, what allows us to manage the stress of competition? How can we perform under pressure?

CHOKING

The problem with trying too hard is that doing so often leads to difficulties. One vivid memory for me occurred when I was finishing a tennis match in a local tournament. Tennis sets are defined by winning six games, but you have to win by two games. If you get to 5–5, you can still win 7–5. In the past, players would just keep playing until someone won two games in a row. You might have heard of the endless tennis match that John Isner played at Wimbledon that ran across several days. At Wimbledon, there was no tiebreak in the fifth and final set. To avoid these endless matches tennis has instituted the tiebreak. Even Wimbledon broke down and instituted a tiebreak at 10–10 in the fifth and final set.

After all the stress of a set, you get to the tiebreak with your nerves fried. The tiebreak is defined by winning seven points. You are both seven points away from making it all count and seven points away from losing it all. The problem is that you have to win two more points than your opponent. Once you get to 6–6, someone has to win two points in a row to take the set. It is also known as sudden death. The feeling of winning and losing literally comes to hinge on every point.

In this particular tournament, I was mired in one of these tie-breaks in the second set. It meant that I was a few points away from winning the whole match. At one point I was in a position to hit a backhand. As my arm swung forward it began to tremble on its own. The rest of my body seemed relatively calm, and I was tired from having played so long. As the ball approached, I began to worry that I would not be able to hit the ball at all. I remember just swinging my arm consciously to try and float the ball anywhere on the court in front of me. I had been playing tennis for a long time. I had hit thousands of backhands just like this one. Like a beginner hitting one of his or her very first backhands, I was relegated to working consciously to make contact. Just getting the ball over the net enough at that point.

We have all experienced a drop in performance when we are playing. To paraphrase John McEnroe, everyone chokes; Grand Slam champions just choke less. To put it a bit more elegantly, no one is immune to a decrement in performance when competing under pressure.

In the book *Choke*, Sian Beilock recalls the time that she was being considered for an advanced club team in soccer. She was ready to play and clearly physically capable of doing well. And then everything began to crumble. She began to play much worse than she expected. She was never able to move up as far as she wanted to in the soccer world.

Of course, we cannot consider her to be a failure. Her experiences fed many of the questions that were central to the work, which culminated in two books and many published articles. After a stint as a professor at the University of Chicago, she became the president of Barnard College and in 2023 became the president of Dartmouth. In the end, things turned out quite well for her.

In her work, Beilock notes that other people seem to thrive under pressure. It seems that the higher the stakes, the better they perform. How is this possible? What makes people resistant to choking? Beilock offers us some ideas about how to work on performing your best. The list can get pretty long. My favorite tip is to find a way to keep your mind focused on something quite small.

To apply this suggestion, one trick I learned was to focus on the flash of the ball on my strings. There is not enough time to really see the ball before the impact on a set of tennis strings. But if I stare at my racket before the ball hits it, I can see the ball as a short flash. By focusing on the flash, I am able to keep my focus on something that occurs in, well, a flash. And in thinking less I am able to let my body do its thing. Being able to limit my focus allowed me to just float the ball using my backhand while my arm was in a nervous fit. Had I lamented my inability to hit a great shot or aspired to even more, like finishing the point outright, I would have most likely missed. Instead, I just focused on simply getting the ball over the net.

Talking about ourselves as if there is more than one person inside of us may seem odd, but it is not without precedent. Ivan Lendl, a Hall of Fame tennis player who won multiple tournaments at all levels, did not start as such a strong player. He lost his first few major tournament finals to the top players of his time. Frustrated, he began to look for anything that would give him an edge.

One way he tried to overcome difficulties during a tennis match was to seek out a sports psychologist. During these sessions, the psychologist taught him to talk about himself in the third person. Lendl would walk around during his everyday life talking about "Ivan doing this and Ivan doing that." When he got on the tennis court, this exercise allowed him to separate that conscious part of his mind form the unconscious one that played tennis.

I am just like everyone else. There were plenty of times that I had an easy shot and just missed it. Once I had set point again in a tiebreak and my opponent was cramping. He could not walk anymore and the whole court was open. I missed the shot. I could have been angry. Instead, I was completely amazed at what I could not do. It's as if you took a walk to your front door and kicked it really hard when you got close and were unable to open it. How can we not walk right up to our front door, stop, and open it?

The battle of our selves has some roots in our neurobiology: the one that tells us what to do and the one that just does it. The problem with the teller is that it often wants to intervene in the doing. It does not trust that the doer will do his or her job. So we work too hard and force the body to do something. As we saw earlier, most of our cortical brain systems are tightly connected to lower-level systems. When it comes to doing, the teller can only give very general instructions. Then it has to leave the doer to do its thing. And herein lies the dilemma. How do we coordinate these two selves? Brain science gives us some answers.

BUILDING COMPLICATED THOUGHTS FROM SIMPLE STARTING POINTS

Our brains are not like a modular home. You don't just pour concrete, build walls, close rooms, add doors, then start to fill in the inside. Our brains have come together over years. Each new system that comes in must contend with getting information from the old systems that were there before it. Imagine that to get to the kitchen you always had to go through the basement since it was built first. And to go upstairs, you would have to go through the basement, the kitchen, then the living room, and finally get to the bedroom. It would be somewhat restrictive. It's as if our brains have very particular ways to transmit information.

Almost all forms of basic motor control are routed through our subcortex. Close your eyes and imagine doing any complex motor task. Imagine swinging a golf club, learning a new dance move, or trying to sing a new tune. In all these cases, creating these higher-level patterns requires going through lower-level circuits. Because of these divisions, it is possible that we can do and sense things that we do not know. Earlier I discussed how I would lose sight of the tennis ball right before contact. Some people lose sight entirely but can still see.

A documented example of seeing but not seeing is called *blindsight*. In this phenomenon, people have damage to the visual centers in the outer layer of the brain at the back of the head. Because there is damage to the areas that receive visual information, they have a hole in their visual field. It is like a massive blind spot. Sometimes the hole is so big that people cannot see on one side of them. When researchers show them a stimulus—for example, a light—in the area where they are blind, they report seeing nothing. Hence, the blind part of blindsight.

Researchers then ask them to guess where the visual stimulus might be. Surprisingly, this brain-impaired blindness can be overcome. People with blindsight still report seeing nothing but guess better than chance where that stimulus is. The way that happens is due to a system that is subcortical. This system takes information from visual pathways. It then creates localization of stimuli in the visual field.

When the cortex is not damaged, both the subcortical and cortical route affect our tracking. The subcortical system is fast, and it gives a first pass to help orient our vision. Shortly thereafter comes the second system, the one in the cortex. Our conscious experience of where things are originates in this cortical system. The subcortical system is actually outside our consciousness.

Only in blindsight can we show vision without consciousness. Earlier I referred to the doer. But in reality it is the senser and doer. These lower-level systems can actually guide us without our knowing it. We can think of this as that doer self, the one that tennis players blame when they miss an easy ball. The question is, who is the teller?

THE OUTER GAMES

So far we have focused on the inner layers, what researchers call the *subcortex*. These areas come online earlier in our lives. The question is what drives the outer game, the parts of the brain that are trying to tell us what to do? To understand this more fully, we can revisit work by Mark Johnson. Johnson was the researcher who took the idea of imprinting in chicks that was popularized by Konrad Lorenz and applied it to human infants.

The two systems, conSpec and conLearn, apply to other things. conSpec, a system that develops very early, points us in the right direction. conLearn, which is in the cortex, starts to take information in from various senses and combines it with motor information. From childhood to adulthood, we encounter one reorganization after the other. We can recognize faces and other objects. Eventually, we use a version of this to read words. As adults we become experts at all sorts of things.

Working with technology must be making our minds more nimble in some way so that we can deal with what feel like constant updates and changes to the devices around us. My wife, Naomi, used to complain about computer programs all the time. I would have to figure out how to help her. Now, she has learned three different electronic medical record systems. She manages social media with no problem, watches YouTube TV without a hitch, and navigates our Apple TV very easily. She can use Zoom and has now figured out how to troubleshoot it. She hated computers but she had no choice but to adapt because they are everywhere. Every car has all kinds of bells and whistles. And I can see the training effect. At times I forget that there was a time when these digital devices fooled her.

What systems are involved in these higher-level types of tasks? How do we tell ourselves to do things? A funny question arises when we think about who is telling whom. So let's reformulate this question a bit: What brain areas are helping us to learn new things? In fact, the answer to this question is a little easier to answer.

FINE-TUNING THE BRAIN

Mark Johnson in his model of brain development argues that with age, the brain becomes more specialized. The route to this specialization in the brain involves changing forms of brain activity. Early in development each area is strongly tied to activity around it.

Let's consider an example from language. Katherine Demuth has focused on how children break up the sounds of a language. English speakers tend to learn a two-syllable envelope that covers two words. So English-speaking children learn "the car" as a single item. Spanish-speaking children on the other hand learn a three-syllable envelope. This covers items such as "el carro." This allows children to learn the grammar of a language by starting to combine sounds. If we were to zoom out and observe the brain, we would see that areas involved in speech would handle this. As the sound patterns build up, the activation of areas in the temporal lobe would start to co-activate more and more.

Areas involved in sensory processing, and later in motor processing, become fine-tuned first. Then, they start to interconnect with other areas. A three-year-old child might be trying to work out how words get put together. Ten years later he or she might be working on speaking to other people while riding a bike. Even later it would involve speaking and driving (with hands free, of course). As language gets embedded with other things the brain areas needed begin to cover more and more real estate.

A similar example comes from Tom Byer's small ball approach. For him, the key to soccer is to manipulate a small ball. His kids learned to walk while pushing a soccer ball around with their feet. You can imagine that the areas involved in doing this would be centered in the motor and sensory areas of the brain. These areas would refine their activity as the children improved. Later, soccer would involve more and more complicated information. At first it might be passing the ball to others and learning to cut passes off. It would evolve to defensive and offensive formations. As adults, high-level players become aware of the clock, their opponent, and the score. All these types of information are progressively more complex and involve wider and wider areas in the brain. Johnson calls this *interactive specialization*, which is the idea that we go from very basic sensory and motor parts of the brain to a much larger interconnected web.

Now we can go back to the senser and doer. The doer in a way is like a childlike—or if we consider evolution—an earlier, more primate-based brain. It involves lower levels of processing, at least for single skills. As we grow older, we can form loops that help us to off-load complicated tasks. In chapter 1, I discussed the fact that chess players could quickly "feel" whether they were in an attacking or defensive position when looking at chess layouts. They knew how to read a chessboard quickly. In most games, chess players could rely on this bank of knowledge to try and win a game. If they were playing an opponent they had played often, they would likely put a strategy in place.

Thus, becoming an expert as an adult involves learning to deal with automatic information. Work with experts has found that early learning of a skill leads to a kind of brain off-loading. Experts tend to use a narrower set of brain areas that are involved in sensing and doing. Nonexperts on the other hand tend to use a lot of different areas of the brain and recruit areas needed for difficult tasks to a greater extent. Of course, this works for familiar situations. Once a situation becomes unfamiliar, everything changes. Even an expert can choke.

PUTTING AN EXPERT TO THE TEST

Garry Kasparov was the champion of champions in his time. In 1984 at the age of twenty-two, he became the youngest world champion at the time. To date only one other champion, Magnus Carlsen, has obtained a higher ranking than him. Kasparov continued a record of dominance against human opponents until 2005, when he retired.

It was his performance in 1997 at the height of his chess-playing career that would come to define him. Garry Kasparov's worst enemy was not a human but an IBM computer called Deep Blue. Deep Blue's only job at the time was to play chess. It was so fast and powerful that it could go through many chess games very quickly. Up until then, no computer had ever beaten a human. Kasparov was intent on winning so that it would stay that way.

The first time they met, Kasparov managed to win. What he figured out very quickly was that Deep Blue played using histori-cal chess games as its base. To defeat Deep Blue, Kasparov played unconventionally. He would try and confuse Deep Blue. In their first encounter, Kasparov's unconventional approach worked.

The second encounter did not go as well. Kasparov is said to have made a key mistake in one of the openings of a game. Some people even suggest that he grew nervous and choked. He denies this claim. Regardless of the outcome, Kasparov found himself having to work extra hard. He could no longer just play using the skills that had worked on his human opponents. In this second game, to win he had to stop relying on instinct and use his prob-lem-solving skills.

Work by Ulrike Basten and Christian Fiebach has focused on brain circuits involved in intelligence tasks. These circuits are in a specific set of brain areas: the inferior parietal lobe and the dorso-lateral prefrontal cortex. These two areas form a circuit that helps join information coming from the senses with information used to make a response. These two areas have been found to come alive during very difficult tasks. Most intellectually challenging tasks in-volve a degree of flexibility. They make us tap into the inner reaches of our memories to try and figure out how to do something new.

These two areas must have been in a neural firestorm in Kasp-arov. He sought ways to beat an opponent more skilled than any he had faced before. Kasparov was one of the very best players at the time. The circuits he used are ones that are necessary when-ever we take on a new task. Even though we can rely on the doer and senser some of the time, we cannot rely on them all the time. Sometimes we need to think, and we need the teller.

If we are lucky, our brains do and tell us the same things. It is the kind of harmonious feeling that leads to the best performance. However, sometimes there is disharmony. We are simply unable to perform at our best. I have suggested focusing on something very small in moments of difficulty. Another strategy might be to talk about ourselves in the third person.

Work by Bastien and her colleagues suggests that it could be a large circuit that is working very hard during these difficult phases. One question we are left with is whether these brain areas are involved in actual physical tasks. In other words, do the rules of cognitive stress apply to physical performance stress?

CONFLICT ON THE FIELD

Hitting a tennis serve under pressure is analogous to another situation in sport: a free kick in soccer. In this situation, it is a person with total control of the ball with his or her feet facing a goalie who can use any means to stop the ball. The kicker stands twelve yards (eleven meters) from the goal in a centered position. The official whistles, the kicker prepares, takes a few steps, and boom. The ball is off. It either goes in the goal, misses the mark, or is blocked by the goalie. The pressure grows greater in elimination matches, where the whole game rides on a bunch of free kicks to the goal.

A recent study looked at brain activity during free goal kicks using a newer technology called *functional near infrared spectroscopy*, or fNIRS. fNIRS essentially beams light into the skull that then bounces off the blood vessels at the surface of the cortex. The light that bounces is read by sensors that detect how much oxygen is in the blood in a particular area.

In this study, the researchers put sensors over the prefrontal cortex, the area that combines information from the senses and motor responses. It is the frontal axis of the circuit that Bastien and her colleagues have associated with IQ tests. The researchers also put sensors over the left motor cortex and the left temporal cortex. Kickers were asked to kick the ball with no goalie, a friendly goalie, and a competitive goalie. To make the stakes higher a gift card was offered to increase the pressure on test subjects in the competitive goalie condition. Both experienced players and less experienced players were tested. Finally, all the players were assessed on how anxious they felt when kicking.

The results showed that anxious players showed more activity in both the prefrontal and motor cortex. It is as if the brain was in conflict, working to allocate more energy to both planning and executing the kick. Inexperienced players showed a difference in the temporal cortex when successfully making a goal. The temporal cortex is related to language, suggesting that talking might help less experienced players.

When the researchers tried to separate the groups using brain signals, they found that both experience and anxiety were correlated with brain activity in the motor areas. The prefrontal cortex was related to scored goals. What we see here is the two selves laid out in the brain. The doer is busy dealing with the execution of the task. The motor cortex moves the body parts that lead to physical effect. At the same time, anxiety also drives the motor cortex. Anxious players require more brain activity to execute the same goal. Meanwhile, the prefrontal cortex is related to how well we execute the motor action.

The battle of the two selves is one that permeates every aspect of tasks that we undertake. As humans, we have to coordinate what we do. This process can be both physical and mental. The fact that the very same areas of the brain are recruited for mental and physical tasks fits very well with the idea of the mind as an extension of the body. Or put more aptly, skills emerge when our brains and bodies work together.

If the physical is mental and the mental is physical, then we can look for more connections between the two. If there are two selves, we can go one step further. What happens when our selves get embedded in a larger network? What happens when our environments change? This is a question that researchers and sports fans alike have been asking themselves as of late. In an earlier chapter, I alluded to the fact that the physical and mental might be related. As we will see next, changes in the environment have an effect on both cognitive and physical tasks.

(14)

CASE STUDY: TOM BRADY, JAMES FLYNN, AND OUR CHANGING ENVIRONMENT

FIFTY IS THE NEW THIRTY

In 2020, the Tampa Bay Buccaneers beat the Kansas City Chiefs in the Super Bowl. Immediately after they won, Tom Brady was named the Greatest of All Time, or GOAT. For much of his career, Brady was associated with Bill Belichick, the head coach of the New England Patriots, where he was the quarterback for six of the nine Super Bowls he played in. His last victory made him 7 for 10. The numbers are staggering and the impressive part is that Brady seems to have retained or improved on his ability to quarterback between the ages of thirty-seven and forty-three.

In the past, many of the great quarterbacks were beaten up physically. For example, Joe Namath retired with knee problems after thirteen years in the NFL. After more than twenty years in the NFL, Brady was still in excellent shape physically. He considered at one point playing until age fifty. When asked about Brady's GOAT status, Jerry Rice, a Hall of Fame wide receiver, noted that the 1980s and '90s, when he played, was a much more physical era.

Brady is accompanied by a number of other "old" quarterbacks in recent years, including Drew Brees (age forty-two), Philip Rivers (thirty-nine), Aaron Rodgers (thirty-nine), and Ben Roethlisberger (thirty-eight). This list raises a question: What is the root cause of this graying of quarterbacks? We could argue that it is genetic. Maybe there are more gifted athletes who are becoming quarterbacks. These better-endowed athletes perform better and keep playing football.

We could also argue that the cause is environmental. During the last few decades, the NFL has changed dramatically. The crisis over concussions and head-to-head collisions has led to a change in rules. Quarterbacks are protected more than ever. Nutrition has improved, and sports science and physical training routines have been altered. The result of this is great quarterbacks playing better and better. It is both a result of the change in environment and the players' own genetic tendencies (height, vision, speed, movement), which feed off each other.

A similar trend can be seen in other sports. In tennis, Roger Federer seemed to be defying the odds by playing high-level tennis at the age of thirty-eight. Unfortunately, he suffered a second knee injury in 2021, and he played his last professional match at the Laver Cup in September 2022. Injury kept him from coming back. Nevertheless, he is one of the oldest players to have a spot in the top ten at the professional level.

His contemporaries, Rafael Nadal and Novak Djokovic, have competed for major tournaments up until the age of thirty-five. Pete Sampras quit at thirty-one, completely burned out physically and mentally. Andre Agassi lasted until he was thirty-five but had to finish his career with the help of cortisone shots in his ailing back. Djokovic, in contrast, was one match shy of winning all four major tournaments in one year at the age of thirty-four. He is healthy and expects to compete for many more years. Of course, the younger generation is gaining ground and losing their fear. They may eventually take over. But when they do, it will be at a much more advanced age relative to past champions.

This increased longevity has also been accompanied with a very high level of performance. At one point Djokovic, Nadal, and Federer stood at twenty major titles each. All three eclipsed Sampras's record of fourteen. Agassi's record of eight majors almost seems like a footnote in the history of tennis. Thus, more modern tennis champions had longer careers with much more success.

In golf, we see a similar trend. Dan McLaughlin started to play in his thirties. In the past, this would have been a very old age to try and become a golf pro. Elite professional golfers, like tennis players, typically began to drop off, albeit a bit later—usually in their mid-forties.

In 2021, this trend changed. Phil Mickelson (fifty-one), Stewart Cink (forty-eight), Lee Westwood (forty-eight), and Richard Bland (forty-eight) remained competitive on the PGA Tour. They might not have hit the ball as hard as younger players, but they seemed to play smarter. They often applied pressure to their younger opponents.

In 2019, at the age of forty-three, Tiger Woods became the second-oldest player to win a major—Jack Nicklaus holds the record for oldest champion at age forty-six. Both Woods and Nicklaus would be considered the elite of the elite. The two of them hold eighteen and fifteen major victories, respectively. Had Woods stayed healthy and not suffered a major car accident, it is very possible that he would have broken Nicklaus's record. The remarkable thing is that more and more players are maintaining a similarly high level in their forties. Whereas Nicklaus was once an outlier, we are left to wonder whether someone older than him will win a major in the near future.

We could consider all kinds of reasons that there have been such dramatic changes in tennis, American football, and golf. It could be many individual factors. But we cannot ignore that Sampras and Agassi inspired the later generation. The same goes for the great quarterbacks. Then the members of the later generation began a race against each other. Woods took inspiration from Nicklaus. Together they reached heights that they would never have reached alone. Federer was so inspired by older players that he created the Laver Cup, a competition between two teams: Europe versus the world. It is named for Rod Laver, Federer's idol, who won all four major tournaments in a calendar year twice. He is the last man to accomplish this feat, first in 1962 and then again in 1969.

This type of generational shift has taken place for amateur athletes as well. In marathon running, runners seem to be sharing training secrets. My oldest daughter, Kiara, is considering running a marathon using a training regimen she found online. With this new outlook, individuals advance themselves but also propel their entire cohort forward. Like two living beings, the individual and environment form an almost symbiotic relationship that not only keeps both beings alive but actually makes them thrive.

DIFFERENCES IN IQ

The idea of IQ is in principle a simple one. An intelligence quotient tells us how intelligent people are—that is, it tells us a person's *psychometric intelligence*. It's a measure of how well people do on a set of standardized tasks that psychometricians use to test IQ. Researchers use many different measures to derive a score and then note the extent to which people deviate either above or below this average. To standardize the score, they set the average to 100 and then scale the scores so that a specific percentage of people fall in certain score ranges. Fifty percent of the test takers score between 90 and 110. About 16 percent score between 80 and 90 and another 16 percent score between 110 and 120. About 7 percent fall into the next 10-point interval above and below, and finally, 2 percent score above 130 or below 70. On this scale, a 15-point increase is the difference between average and high average.

Work on IQ was at the forefront of psychological research for almost the entire twentieth century. The interesting part is the role played by a complete outsider who just happened to be looking at

IQ data. This outsider was James Flynn, a political scientist. Yes, that is right: a political scientist is responsible for one of the most significant discoveries in psychological science. His findings were so revolutionary that he had an effect named after him, the Flynn Effect.

You might wonder why a political scientist was working on IQ, a measure used in psychology and education. IQ became heavily politicized during the twentieth century. We can thank Arthur Jensen—at least during that period—for the politicization of IQ. Jensen's work focused mostly on measuring and analyzing IQ data and was not concerned with race at all. His most significant advancement in the field was finding a way to create a composite for IQ, a general score the captured what was common to all IQ tests.

At that point, Jensen's work was not considered controversial. However, in creating this general score, Jensen naturally began to look at different studies that looked at IQ. This led him to consider how genetics, which he associated with IQ differences, in turn related to education. Jensen learned of Audrey Shuey's work along these lines. In Shuey's review of 382 studies, he found that there was a clear IQ gap between Black and White children in the United States. Jensen took this data, ran it through his statistical meat cleaver, and came to the conclusion that somewhere between 50 and 75 percent of the variance in IQ differences between races was due to genetic factors.

Jensen identified two different types of processing. Level I processing could be seen in memorization using rote methods, something like just playing back a recording. Tasks that tap into this level of processing are best captured in word-list learning, in which people are given a list of words and asked to study them. After some time, subjects are asked to recall as many words as they can. Level I processing could also be seen in activities like spelling, learning math facts, or memorizing lyrics.

Level II processing would be much more complex and involve what we would call cognitive tasks—tasks like generalizing from one set of items to a principle. For example, if I ask you to point out what three words have in common (e.g., rough, beer, cold), that would be considered a more cognitive task. Other examples include algebra and higher mathematics, achieving scientific and technological innovations, and inventing something new. Level I intelligence might allow people to do somewhat well on an IQ test. However, Jensen noted that in recent years, level II intelligence had become more and more important for IQ scores. These higher cognitive abilities would allow one to deduce that *draft* is the word that connects *rough*, *beer*, and *cold* together. By using cognitive processing, we would see that *rough draft, draft beer*, and *cold draft* would lead us to the correct answer. In Jensen's view, these more difficult tasks that were measured in IQ tests were determined by genetic differences. Following his logic, Black and White children differed on IQ tests due to genetic differences.

OUR CHANGING ENVIRONMENT

When Flynn began to look at IQ data across time he realized that something was appearing that did not fit with Jensen's assertion. IQ appeared to be rising about three points every decade, which would lead to about a fifteen-point change in fifty years. The data led Flynn to a very different conclusion than the one proposed by Jensen. He consequently proposed a statistical argument that pushed back against Jensen's assertions. His argument is pretty simple. Genetic effects do not happen overnight. These changes are on the scale of hundreds or thousands of years. The fifteen-point rise in IQ cannot be due to genetic changes. However, during this fifty-year period the IQ for populations from the most industrialized countries rose from average to high average.

Flynn noted that the improvement appeared in nonverbal IQ, which involves extraction of visual patterns without a lot of language. You can see this in our interactions with technology. I think about computer programs we use or even the interfaces of our digital devices. It used to be that I could tell the percentage of battery left on my phone. Before, the percentage of battery was on the battery icon in the top right corner of my old iPhone 8's screen. Now I have to swipe down from the top right on my iPhone X to see it. I used to have a home screen that looked like all my other screens. Now my home screen has icons, and my other screens have a bunch of folder-like collections of different programs, or applications as they are called now.

I can also pull from the top to search for an application. If I want to know the weather or the latest headlines, I pull from the right middle side of the screen when I turn it on. I can control my lights with the hue app, send messages with Microsoft Teams, manage my lab with Monday, and so on.

This need to think about what I'm doing all the time is similar to what happened to me when I went to Germany for a year. I did not just have to use German. I had to learn to tell the difference between fifty-cent, twenty-cent, one-euro, and two-euro coins. I had to stand in line differently. Even the doors there work differently. I also drove about ten different types of cars and drove through five different countries. At the end of that year, coming back to the United States seemed easy. I didn't have to think about what I was doing all the time. As I noted earlier, my wife Naomi has had a similar experience with technology.

All this environmental change is what has led to the steady rise in IQ. Dickens and Flynn conclude that "results have shown how the reciprocal causation of phenotypic IQ and environment could mask, multiply, and average environmental effects, so that relatively small environmental influences could produce large changes in IQ."

In that quote, we see it all: small differences in the environment snowball across time. People use technology more; they then invent newer and newer forms of technology, which in turn changes how they interact with their devices, and so on and so forth. All these very small changes in the environment feed on themselves across time, leading to what appear to be effects that Jensen attributed to heredity.

What Flynn is implicitly arguing is an emergentist view of IQ. It's similar to a point that Tom Byer made with soccer. Byer's program did not focus purely on individuals. He argued that changes were generational. Improvement actually trickles up. As the lowest-performing levels improve, they put pressure on the next-highest level. These changes at a cohort level eventually change generations. In reality the whole behavioral approach to genetics misses one crucial aspect of human abilities. We can create averages or try to extract a linear measure for understanding how human abilities change over time. However, changes are nonlinear. They mushroom and grow without following a straight line.

The approach of measurement focuses on only a small part of what is actually going on. Measurement to some extent involves an inner individual-level game, focused on a particular task we are trying to accomplish. In the end doing this is like trying to describe the world using only flat surfaces. We can try to do it, but we will miss something.

The changes in individual IQ triggered by general environmental changes is the result of an outer game. Teilhard de Chardin would see this as a layer of human culture, the noosphere, that surrounds our planet. It is a product of the roundness of the earth, the way in which organisms interact and transform our world. It is this emergent form that plays a principal role in the world and our relationship to it.

Being connected to something larger is also the feeling that comes when we engage in a task. In some cases, it can propel us forward. Perhaps most amazing are individuals who found a road to improvement in the darkest of times. Under very dire circumstances, it was a connection to something larger than themselves that led them forward.

15

EVOLUTION, REVOLUTION, AND THE PATH TO SKILL DEVELOPMENT

FROM DARKNESS FLOWS LIGHT

The ravages of World War II left millions dead, and those who survived were in virtual poverty. Those involved in the war—regardless of which side of the conflict—lost loved ones. Particularly gruesome was the internment and murder of millions of European Jews. They were stripped of their belongings and shipped to camps where they worked hard labor under the threat of ending up in a human gas chamber. Those who did not die of starvation or were killed suffered other horrible fates. It would be hard to suggest that a positive light could be placed on such a vicious and bloody war. And yet one man was able to find hope in such a hopeless experience.

One of the best books I have ever read has this most gruesome of backstories. From a concentration camp during the Holocaust comes one of the most positive stories, one that would be read by people all over the world. It is *Man's Search for Meaning* by Victor Frankl. In it he details his experiences during his time in a concentration camp.

When I read it in English as a young adult, it was inspiring. Recently, I bought a newer edition in German with a foreword by Hans Weigel, an Austrian writer and critic. Weigel, who was Jewish, fled to Switzerland during the Nazi annexation of Austria, thereby avoiding the fate of those who were not able to flee with him. The foreword reveals his amazement at Frankl's resilience.

Frankl had climbed the academic ladder from the position of *dozent*, or lecturer, all the way up to professor. In 1938, he was extremely well known and had given lectures in many halls in Vienna. Weigel notes that Frankl, like many Jewish Austrians, lost everything with the Nazi annexation. While at the concentration camp in Auschwitz, Victor Frankl was asked to work day after day under the most dire of conditions. His description of such a desolate experience also contains hope. Somehow amid all this loss, many people were able to hang on to something to keep their spirits alive. The description below is particularly telling:

> It came one time this way. One night when we were dead tired from work, our soup spoons in hand, strung out on the floor of the barracks, one of our fellow prisoners summoned us. Through the exhaustion and the cold air, outside we could see the view of the sunset not completely gone. Once outside we saw the glowing clouds in the west and the fantastic forms and the celestial steel blue color and the glowing blood red just below it which was reflected in the puddles on the ground. After several minutes of silence, he asked all of us, "How much more beautiful can this world truly be?"

In this quote, Frankl notes how even in the darkest of times, he could enjoy the beauty of nature and feel connected to something much larger than himself. So could all the others who witnessed such stunning vibrant colors in the sky during one of the most horrific periods of their lives.

Thirty-eight years later, it was this positivity that was the topic of Frankl's lecture in the Wiener Hofburg, one of the halls that had been the venue for a lecture he had given as a respected scholar before the war in 1938. His experiences had led him to establish a form of psychotherapy that sought a humanistic way out of people's psychological difficulties. He called it *logotherapy*. *Logos* means "reason" in Greek. His idea was that pain and suffering are tolerable only when they have meaning and when there is purpose to our lives.

FLOWING ACROSS A NETWORK

World War II also left Mihaly Csikszentmihalyi disappointed with the reality that adults had created for themselves. While Frankl was in a concentration camp, Csikszentmihalyi was a child growing up in war-torn Italy. Csikszentmihalyi stumbled upon his area of research because of his own experience during World War II, in which he lost family to the war and lost his family's possessions. These experiences naturally led him to question whether a different way of life could be forged.

Like Frankl, Csikszentmihalyi felt that psychology could help him find the answer. He enrolled in psychology classes but found that most of the work focused on looking at how reinforcement led rats to look for food in a maze. He reasoned that if the only thing that was of value to the rats was food, then they would behave exactly the way they did. However, humans were different. As humans we have a whole world open to us. He sought to look at people who were doing something that was not necessary. That is when his research took him to artists.

When he first began to study artists, he noticed something very odd. Artists would spend huge amounts of time painting, completely absorbed in their work. They would finish a painting and then immediately begin a new one. When he interviewed them, he realized that they were more interested in the act of painting than in the completed painting. He wondered if this attitude was specific to artists.

He began to search for other venues where he might find people who were fully engaged in a task. He repeatedly found that people reported the feeling of being lost in an activity without regard to the outcome. They did so no matter what country they came from. He termed this feeling *flow*.

Flow is the concept of losing oneself in an activity with no other purpose than the enjoyment of that activity. It happens in all kinds of different venues: at work, when playing instruments, when playing sports, and even, in some cases, at school. If we go back to Frankl's experience during the sunset, we could call it flow. We might also recognize it in Tom Byer's approach to teaching soccer, and even in Ericsson's thinking of deliberate practice.

I have not preached much in this book but let me add my two cents on the dilemma facing Ericsson, the notion that deliberate practice and measurement are the primary way to measure our improvement in skill. They might be, but let me offer another answer. The way to measure how well we are doing is to determine whether we get lost in an activity. The more we get lost, the more likely we will find purpose and meaning in simply doing it. And the more this happens the better we will get.

Work on flow also fits in with current work in neuroscience. Brain scanning techniques have shown that multiple brain networks interface with a self-network. Across many studies conducted over many years there always appears to be a network that consistently shows more activity when people are *not* doing a task. This network is called the *default network*. This main area is the ventromedial prefrontal cortex, which lies in the middle part of the frontal lobe toward the very front of the brain. These networks consist of both a self-network and other networks devoted to various types of activity that we undertake.

Earlier we talked about the connection between the prefrontal cortex and the parietal lobe, which is especially valuable for tasks that are difficult and require working memory. If like a former student of mine you were to try to simultaneously drive, eat a banana split, and switch gears (yes, it was a manual transmission), then the network consisting of these two areas would be important in trying to coordinate multiple actions in the right order. Earlier I speculated that it might have been the network that Kasparov used to try to fool Deep Blue. Other networks focus on our internal physical states and on external social circumstances, among others. The main point of this study was the notion of the self in context. The self can be seen as the experience we are having. The context is our views of the past, present, and future.

The notion of a network within the brain is interesting in light of the view of networks in general as proposed by Albert-László Barabási. Barabási suggests that everything is the product of a network. If we extend his ideas to the current discussion, these networks exist at varying levels both within ourselves and outside ourselves. Teilhard de Chardin talks about the way in which this evolution might lead us forward. He talks about the Omega Point, the point at which humans approach their highest level of consciousness. Being bent on trying to integrate his views on theology with those on evolution, he proposed that this highest level was similar to the idea of reaching God. Interestingly, Frankl and Csikszentmihalyi also both discuss a connection to something that is greater than us. It is in these moments of losing ourselves to something larger that people are able to engage in a task and excel beyond their limits. The notion of networks takes the emphasis away from our own progress and improvement. Rather, it helps us to look at how we affect and are affected by all of those who surround each one of us.

THE DAN PLAN REVISITED

The book began by considering the Dan Plan as the ultimate test of Ericsson's view on deliberate practice. Dan did practice, and he tried to implement the plan with supervision by Ericsson himself.

His progress was impressive. Over time he was able to progress significantly, to the point of reaching a very high handicap. To achieve his goals, he practiced for many hours a day. Then his back gave out. He got hurt and his golf career ended.

How is it that someone with little athletic experience and simple determination could achieve so much in such a short time? Ericsson would argue that it is practice that gets us there.

I have argued for most of this book that we need a better understanding of how skills emerge from the combination of small abilities. We even considered what innate might mean by looking at a skill that is present at birth, like the tracking of faces, which is a form of human imprinting. However, even when we can look at what is present at birth there are two important things to note. The face recognition system we are born with serves more like a system that alerts us to what is important. The heavy work requires time and builds on this very early knowledge. Second, a lot of our advanced skills—such as playing chess, mastering a new sport, reading, or learning a new language—don't just build on these basic skills. These advanced skills reshuffle them.

Furthermore, the information that is handled across more and more complex networks changes over time. These networks are both external and internal. If we add the ideas of Teilhard de Chardin, we introduce the idea of transformation, metamorphosis. Mastery, which starts as an emergence of skill, becomes an emergence of self and a reverberation across the many networks that we as individuals inhabit.

FILLING THE GULF

I have spent a lot of time playing tennis. I actually enjoyed tinkering with my game and constantly refining it. Competition gave me an outlet for any frustration that I might be carrying around with me. It also gave me a connection to my family and then later to my kids.

When I turned forty and took it upon myself to improve my game, I didn't just work on the serve. I worked on my entire game. I soon stumbled on the website Tennis Mind Game, which was hosted by Tomaz Mencinger. I bought a small tennis strategy e-book with the hopes that it would let me in on some big *secret* about how to become a great tennis player. My thinking was that the great players had some special strategy that worked for them. I quickly discovered that there was no secret. In fact, most of what they did was pretty predictable and dull. The flashy things are just what stand out for us in our recollections of previous matches.

Besides stressing the mental game, Mencinger also had a lot of videos and drills to help develop people's tennis skills. Over the next few years, he and I exchanged emails about different aspects of the game. What became clear to me during these exchanges was that playing tennis required a very different approach to how I had been operating. I conducted all kinds of experiments. In one case, I tried to stay calm and focused in one practice match and then compared that to trying to play with more intensity and anger in another. Surprisingly, the outcomes were often very similar. Being focused and angry did not result in my winning important points. If anything, it made things worse. So I wondered why I should expend all that energy if it didn't make a difference. This was just one of many things I learned.

The most important lesson was when Tomaz came to Houston and stayed at our house for a few days in 2013. During this visit, Kamille, who was seven, was already starting to play more. Tomaz patiently hit with and guided my kids. His ability to figure out how to improve my children's strokes amazed me. On that day, he began with my two oldest children, Nikolas and Kiara. I saw him pretty quickly clean up their strokes, while I felt unable to grasp all the concepts he was throwing at me.

After he was done, I sent Nikolas and Kiara to another court. When I looked over, Nikolas and Kiara were engaged in a one-sided sibling rivalry. In their typical fashion, Nikolas was being hypercompetitive and trying to win every point he played. Kiara kept breaking up his rough edges. Her lightheartedness thwarted all of Nikolas's attempts to take their ball exchanges too seriously.

On the second court, Kamille and I were hitting and Tomaz was playing the role of orchestra leader. He was helping Kamille do some very basic things. I was concentrating hard, trying to absorb all the information that Tomaz was giving her. Soon he would be flying back to Slovenia, and I would once again be alone trying to lead my kids up the tennis ladder. The pressure to try and get them to play their very best was palpable to me. I desperately wanted them to be really good, and maybe get a college tennis scholarship if they could. But watching Tomaz quickly adjust all our games through exercises and drills was jaw-dropping. He not only had answers for all my questions but his answers would generate two or three more questions. I was desperately trying to find the key that would help me propel my kids forward.

At one point, I told Tomaz that there was an overwhelming amount of work left to do. A huge gap existed between where I wanted my kids to be and where they were at that point. More importantly, I knew I did not have all the answers like a lifelong coach might have. As my head spun, Tomaz must have taken pity on me. He looked over at me and said, "You don't notice it right now, but the nicest thing is that all of you are out playing tennis together. Look at how happy you all are and what a nice day it is." He helped put the emphasis on how enjoyable this moment was for all of us. He was like my own personal Teilhard de Chardin, Frankl, or Csikszentmihalyi reminding me that I should stop and smell the roses. We were indeed lucky to all be sharing that moment together. In fact, today I have no idea what drills he taught me that day or what small mechanical aspect of tennis I learned about. Out of the pursuit of improved skill had come the company of a good friend and a treasured moment with my three children. It took Tomaz's observation for me to notice that. Now years later it is only the beauty of that moment that has stuck with me.

It turns out that I was not the only one looking to the skies and connecting with a larger world. This type of greater connection would be the driving force behind Guillermo Morales, who would stumble by pure chance on his area of expertise, marathon running.

16

FINAL CASE STUDY: THE TEACHINGS OF DON MEMO, AN EMERGENTIST'S PATH TO IMPROVEMENT

THE ROAD FROM IMMIGRANT JANITOR TO MARATHON RUNNER

Guillermo "Memo" Pineda Morales stumbled onto his own version of the Dan Plan. Memo began to run after moving to the United States from Mexico as a young man. In his native town of Santa Ana Coatepec, Mexico, Memo had practiced running informally. At first when he ran, it was to get away from his father, who was a stern man who often scolded and hit Memo. To avoid his father's recriminations, Memo would run. Eventually, he outran his father.

When he reached the sixth grade, Memo's family could not afford to pay for additional schooling. So like many people in his town, he went to work in the fields. Working in the fields would have been his fate if destiny had not intervened. His sister had moved to the United States to work. With the blessing of his mother and $500 that his sister spent to arrange transport with a *coyote*—the Mexican word for a person who is essentially a human trafficker—he made his way to the United States. When he reached the border he ran, and he was able to avoid the authorities.

He made his way to New York, where he worked at whatever job was available. Eventually, he ended up in a factory that was raided by US Immigration and Customs Enforcement (ICE). This time he chose not to run. He spent time in jail and ended up in Louisiana, but with a lawyer he was able to escape deportation.

He returned to New York and began to work again. That is when he began to run in earnest. Memo kept getting better. His training regimen was bare-bones: no fancy gym, no yoga mat to stretch on, and no sophisticated equipment to track his running. As he trained, he imagined being in his hometown. He felt liberated by the fresh air and the outdoors.

When he began to compete, he did surprisingly well. And he just kept getting better, until a car hit him and shattered his knee. The injury forced Memo to stop running. Instead he went to cheer his friends on. As painful as it was for him to watch, it was more painful to run. Then his mother, who was on her deathbed, intervened. She told him to do the thing he loved, even if it meant finishing in last place.

So Memo began to run again. But he never finished in last place. He was able to recover from his injury. As of 2020, Memo was still getting better.

THE EMERGENT CYCLE OF IMPROVEMENT
LEADS TO TRANSFORMATION

In this book, there have been plenty of examples of the ways in which lots of little things add up into something much larger. We can also see this in the story of Memo. Like Tom Byer, Memo did not grow up in a place that favored his particular skill. Both men chose sports that were not particularly suited to their environments. They both kept at them for quite some time. They both pieced together a plan based on observation and their own intuitions.

Tom's and Memo's similarities extend beyond the sports they chose. Both avoided explicit measurements. When Byer returned to the United States, the staff at US Soccer asked him for explicit measurements. But Byer had no need for the quants to measure progress at the individual level. Memo learned to use his body's own signals. Byer looked at how each generation performed. Memo ran with the idea that his ancestors were running with him. He carried images of his childhood home. Both Byer and Memo became much more than they ever anticipated they would.

At this point, you might wonder whether deliberate practice and genetics do not matter after all. To argue that they do not matter would be foolish. Tom Byer clearly had a good enough body to play soccer. Memo had a runner's blessing. His hometown is at a high altitude—a huge bonus for distance runners, who get natural endurance training, especially when their ancestors have lived in those conditions for centuries.

But Memo was a worker first. Running was an escape. It was a part of his life that was integrated into the rest of it. He would stretch in the basement rather than at a fancy gym. Tom Byer thought that good soccer should focus on protecting the ball. The ball should be fully integrated into a child's actions as he or she walked.

Both men had the opportunity to practice their sport. Without official sponsorships, Memo was able to make his way to the London marathon. Had he stayed home, worked the fields, and lived in his hometown where there were scant resources, we might never have seen him run. Byer left for Japan, where he eventually was given a chance to create a program that would take the country from backwater to elite status in the world.

Deliberate practice and genetics contribute to the way in which each of us practices and learns. But there is so much more to mastery than that. For one, we have to be flexible. Ash Barty, who stalled in her ascension of the women's tennis ranking system, decided to take time off and play cricket. When she came back, she improved dramatically. The time away helped to consolidate a new path that propelled her forward.

What we see in all these stories is a cycle of improvement. Yes, we can focus on a particular skill—such as Dan's handicap,

Memo's running times, and Ash Barty's forehand and serve. But each one of these skills is itself like a flower that blooms. It shows our growth. As humans, we are blessed with the ability to continually improve. But our improvement rarely goes in a straight line. And it does not go straight up or down. We are expert improvisers.

In thinking about genetics, researchers working on IQ found that environments can operate on entire populations. James Flynn's initial observations, which involved very small irregularities, eventually led to his discovering that IQ changed dramatically over time. In this view, technological changes across a large segment of society are a form of nonverbal IQ training. The unusual thing is that Flynn was trained as a political scientist, and his discovery of IQ changes was unplanned. His own career path took a shift from one area of research to a completely different one. A political scientist is now credited with an important discovery outside his main field of study. Another hallmark of mastery is how skills blend and shift across time.

My hope is that you will continue focusing on the little things that are needed on your own paths to improvement. We all need to improve a tennis stroke, a golf swing, the way in which we make music, or our chess games. Like Flynn we might notice what looks like a small blip. At first it might seem trivial. Small blips at times can become much more. Little things when gathered together are likely to give us much more than we anticipated. If our greatest gift is these emergent abilities, then we must make sure to look at the larger picture. It is important to consider how each added skill blends into what we already are while also taking us in new directions.

We might think of Memo Morales as Don Memo. He is like a shaman teaching us about the things that will take us farther. More than fifty years ago, Carlos Castañeda met his own shaman, Don Juan Asus, a Yaqui Indian who guided him in a different direction. Don Juan helped guide Castañeda to see a new reality. At the end of their first journey together, Don Juan gave Castañeda advice on how to navigate the complexity of life. Don Juan told him to focus on a path with "a heart." And he told him to traverse it to its full extent. As a traveler, he suggested observing it "breathlessly."

On our human journey, the ability to learn new things, to innovate from small things to much larger things, is our path. Our only job is to learn to traverse it with a heart, to allow ourselves to be absorbed by it. It is in these moments when we are absorbed by these tasks that we enter a state of flow, the state of flow that Csikszentmihalyi described and that Frankl was able to tap into during the most difficult period of his life. This flow can be thought of like Teilhard de Chardin's Omega Point, the moment in which we as humans transcend the physical reality of our world and become our best selves. Whether you are running, playing music, playing chess, reading, or noticing a little blip, seek out this flow. And then enjoy it "breathlessly."

CONCLUSION

Five Principles of Mastery

FROM DROPOUT TO TECH WHIZ

James H. Clark could be thought of as the Anti-Dan. He grew up with little money in a single-parent household that he describes as poorer than poor. His father left when he was a child. His mother, unaware that she could get social assistance, ended up putting the family through extreme hardship. He had no savings to fall back on, never dreamed of enrolling in grad school, and did not have the ability to plan his educational future. He was an abysmal student who frequently acted out at school. He once used his vast intellect to arrange for firecrackers to go off in a classmate's locker. He and the public school district he was enrolled in agreed on just one thing, that he should leave it permanently. A year from graduation he decided to enlist in the navy. Since he was still seventeen, he had to convince his mother to sign the papers that would allow him to enlist.

His adjustment to military training was not completely smooth. Like all recruits, Clark was given a multiple-choice test that would allow him to be placed into high school equivalency classes. He had never taken a multiple-choice test. He read each question and then saw multiple answers below. To him each question was partially right, so he circled all of them. He then turned in his test with all the answers circled.

Upon receiving his exam, the graders immediately suspected that Clark was trying to cheat. One of the ways to fool the computer was to circle all the answers. He was relegated to performing the most demeaning work on the ship. The other crew members would make fun of him. Many would purposefully drop food trays in front of him and then proceed to insult him while he picked them up.

During this time, he became a self-described loan shark. He had gone from extreme poverty at home to the lowest rung of the social hierarchy in the navy. But someone must have had pity on him because after a few months, the officers felt they should try to do something to improve his scholarly skills. Despite his deficient scores, they put him in a few classes. He found solace in school, which was the perfect antidote to the physically nauseating work of the mess hall. He didn't love his classes at first but slowly he grew to appreciate them.

He was particularly interested in an algebra class, where he got the highest score in a class of several dozen people. Clark describes this experience as not only teaching him that he was good at algebra but also as helping him to gain confidence. It turned out that Clark had a natural ability for solving math problems that he never knew about. Little did he know how far this skill would take him.

Shortly after he took the algebra class, he was asked to teach it. Clark had never taken notes when he was a student. Rather than write things down, he would listen carefully. This approach worked as he continued to excel in his classes. He got his choice of duty station and went to the East Coast of the United States. Eventually, he ended up in Louisiana, where he was discharged at the age of twenty-one. In Louisiana he once again enrolled in night school, where he took a finite math course and got an A. He then took an English course and a differential calculus course and got As.

As he grew older, Clark married and began a family. He also took his second chance at getting an education very seriously. He took a job in order to provide for his family. At the same time, he enrolled in night classes at Texas Tech. He notes that his GPA was not the highest, since he had to juggle work, family, and school. But his GPA got him another job back in Louisiana working for Boeing.

While at Boeing, he stumbled on a computer that was running twenty-four hours a day. What Clark noticed was that the computer itself was not the problem. The problem was that it was using a tape drive that was slowing down how quickly the information was stored and accessed. With the help of a manual, Clark was able to get the computer to do the same work using a hard drive that was sitting idly nearby. With the modifications he was able to make the computer do the same work as before in two and a half hours. This accomplishment was so helpful that the company rewarded him. He was given a "zero defects award," which allowed him to work on whatever projects he wanted. So he spent his time at work studying and learning.

Eventually, his interest in math and science allowed him to enroll in graduate school, and he left Boeing to enroll in the University of Utah. There he met Ivan Sutherland, who became his doctoral adviser. Sutherland was an excellent computer scientist in his own right. Before moving to the University of Utah, he had been at Harvard University and also served as the head of the US Defense Department Advanced Research Project Agency's Information Processing Techniques Office. After completing his PhD, he took an assistant professor position at UC Santa Cruz and eventually an associate professor position at Stanford. While at Stanford, he and his students cofounded Silicon Graphics, which would eventually become the provider of visual effects for much of the film industry.

The rest of Clark's career sounds like a list of tech successes. He founded Netscape, the first web browser, as a result of his frustration with Silicon Graphics, which he thought was quickly falling behind the curve. The computers produced by Silicon Graphics were too expensive and the upcoming PC powered by Microsoft was quickly outpacing the Silicon Graphics products. Clark deliberately tried to sabotage his successful company. In his view, the company was already behind the curve. It needed to die and be reborn. But the "suits" would not allow that. So Clark took another extended leave, this time to New Zealand on a secondhand boat he had bought. There, some of the Silicon Graphics engineers who were equally frustrated with the way the company and its product were evolving helped him to rethink computing.

Back home from his sabbatical, Clark rode his motorcycle and crushed the tibia in his leg. Relegated to bed rest, he wrote a paper titled "The Telecomputer." In his view, this new computer would allow people to talk to each other. Many companies began to invest lots of dollars in the project. But Clark moved on before it ever got off the ground.

When he learned about Mosaic, one of the first web browsers, Clark realized the next big industry would not involve his original idea of a telecomputer. He realized that each computer needed to be controlled by each user. This new product, Netscape, the first web browser, would lay the groundwork for a whole new digital world. When you read the history of the Internet, social media, and our networked world, Clark's name is prominent.

Clark's story seems to fly in the face of the view that practice makes perfect. How can it be that a teenager who ended up in the mess hall could get a PhD in physics and then go on to become a successful businessman? No one would pay to grow up the way he did. And yet, we are left wondering if somehow his path is what led him to the top. Or was he somehow different? And if he was different, would we use the word *talent*, a word Ericsson rejects, to describe his hidden ability?

Clark is clearly an outlier. However, his story carries lessons for all of us with an eye toward mastery. No matter what our task might be, his journey sheds light on achievement that goes beyond what seems possible given the starting point. In his story and others in this book we can see the five principles of mastery: *voluntad*, *habilidad*, *oportunidad*, *flexibilidad*, and *claridad*.

PRINCIPLE 1: *VOLUNTAD*

Voluntad, or "will." Mastery starts with some simple questions:
What do you enjoy doing? What are the things that you would like
to do?

James H. Clark touches on an important theme that we have
considered in this book. How do we choose what it is that we
should master? Clark thought he was terrible at school. In the navy,
he flunked his first test. Then he found out that he was a pretty
good student. It is clear from this story that he was pretty willful.
Whereas this will was the source of his troubles in school, it also
became the force that led to success.

As he became interested in electronics, he realized that he could
study science and eventually obtain a PhD in physics. A similar twist
occurred with Jane Goodall, who loved her stuffed gorilla. How could
a child turn her love for a stuffed gorilla into a career? Almost every
case study we have seen is about someone who wanted to do something and gravitated to it naturally. In our own pursuit of mastery, I
think considering what we like to do is important.

Sometimes will is also needed to overcome obstacles. There are
things that we will have to do that are not things we always like
to do. I don't really like jogging in the heat. But at some point I
had to do it if I wanted to play tennis. In fact, I learned to battle
through the hot southeastern Texas summers on the court so successfully that people began to think I *liked* the heat. I hate it but
it is something I have to do to play tennis, which I do love. Later
when I tore my meniscus, I had to use an off-loading brace, which
helped to alleviate my pain. When I walk onto the court, people
look at me with concern. Sometimes I leave the brace on for the
rest of the day. If I am out in public, I get all kinds of stares. It
doesn't bother me. After all, I have to thank this brace for giving
me another chance to play the game I love.

It all starts with our will. *Voluntad* is the key to taking our first
steps toward mastery.

PRINCIPLE 2: *HABILIDAD*

Habilidad. To achieve mastery, we have to have some ability in our area of interest. Our ability may not always appear easily. Sometimes we need to figure things out. Clark figured out that he was good at math and physics. Ramón y Cajal became a very good illustrator. Memo Morales became a great marathon runner. Tom Byer went from professional soccer player to skills coach.

The second step on the road to mastery is figuring out what you are able to do. To do this we have to try a few things until we are able to find what it is that we are good at. My very best class in college was physical anthropology. In fact, I loved evolution. I just understood it and it is the only class in which I earned an A+. People thought I was a graduate student when I showed up at a seminar by one of the faculty and asked a few questions. It took me a while but I finally figured out that I really like thinking about how things change over time. Since there is no class on change over time, it took me a while to figure that out.

In your own journey, you can ask yourself questions. Has anyone praised you for something? Maybe they like your pies or think your photographs are good? Do you regularly resolve people's disputes? Are you good with finances and planning? Did you build a home-made computer cabinet during vacation? Do you love watching sports, reading books, playing video games? Video games are now part of a growing profession. You can go to college on a video game scholarship. As time goes on, your interests may change. Like Dan, you may go from golf to setting up a business. Every one of us has an ability that can be developed. Finding yours is another key on your path to mastery.

PRINCIPLE 3: *OPORTUNIDAD*

Oportunidad. We all need a chance. Sometimes it comes in the most unexpected way. When James H. Clark enlisted in the navy, he never imagined that he would come out with an interest in electronics, science, or physics. The navy gave him the chance to take classes. In conversations with colleagues, friends, or even tennis opponents who remain friendly after the heat of the battle, I often hear the same story: someone or something opened up the opportunity for them to try something. One example that I often think of as "what if" is the story of my cousin Michel Corpi, who formed the part of a duo called Cortello. You have probably never heard of them. They put out a Spanish-language album that to my biased ears sounded as good as anything on the radio at the time. The duo wanted to move from San Luis Potosí, Mexico, to Mexico City to pursue their dreams. They never did. However, I saw an opportunity that they never capitalized on. When Michel and Cortello's manager (who is the rapper on one of their singles) came to visit us in Houston in 2012, they mentioned that many groups wanted to buy their songs or have them write songs for them. The manager adamantly stood by the notion that Cortello would become a household name. Well, they are not. And to me the opportunity to write songs for Luis Miguel, Reik, and other much more famous artists at the time was an opportunity. My kids tell me to not focus so much on this lost opportunity.

An opportunity can also be golden. Jane Goodall was given the chance to spend time in Africa, and that eventually led to her attending graduate school. Ash Barty was accepted into tennis lessons at a much younger age than was common at her local tennis club. If we keep our eyes open, we can spot an opportunity. At times an opportunity may come and go, and that brings me to the next principle, flexibility.

PRINCIPLE 4: *FLEXIBILIDAD*

Flexibilidad. If there is one thing that James H. Clark is not, it is stuck. Michael Lewis in his book *The New New Thing* describes him as a man in constant motion. In a way, we can see how this might be antithetical to what school teaches most children. The idea is to be conventional, to learn what we are taught, and then repeat it later, sometimes verbatim on a test. Clark was so disruptive that the school system basically spit him out after finding him unchewable and unpalatable.

His incredible flexibility—the trait that did not allow him to adhere to traditional schooling—led him to abandon things when they were on their way up. He would spot an idea, follow it through, and then let it go. Whereas I would not recommend such an extreme unconventional approach for most people, there are many things to gain from Clark's flexible approach.

Yes, we will all get stuck, and our progress even in the best of circumstances will come to a halt. Even with all the will, ability, and an opportunity, things change. Dan eventually shifted to a new plan when his back gave out. Roger Federer, a throwback who was playing with a racket much smaller than everyone else's, eventually changed to a larger racket head. Pete Sampras did not. Cortello, the musical duo that my cousin Michel was a part of, stuck with their own plans of fame. Maybe they would have been great songwriters. There will come a point when we reach a juncture and need to adapt. This is simply part of the process, and it is important to not be too rigid. Children are notorious for trying things out, as my son did when he complained that the electric socket "bit" him. As we grow older we can sometimes forget to try something different. Humans excel at adapting to new conditions. Ash Barty left tennis and then came back. If you are stuck, it might be worth trying to do something radically different for a little while. Sometimes tapping into this flexibility can help us gain a new perspective. With this changed perspective might come something new and unexpected. Once we shift it is important to observe what is happening. That leads us to the final principle, *claridad*.

PRINCIPLE 5: *CLARIDAD*

Clarity is by far the hardest principle. It requires us to ask ourselves what really matters to us. People often ask me if their kids should be raised bilingual, and if so, when they should learn their second language. My answer is always the same. What is your goal? If you want to raise someone who can speak, read, and write in two languages, certain things have to be put into place at certain ages. This will also depend on what the two languages are. If you want them to learn to read and write in Mandarin and their first language is English, it will be a long process that most likely has to start at a young age. If it is a Romance language, then you can start a bit later if you are an English speaker. Even monolingual English-speaking adults can learn to write pretty well in a Romance language.

Tom Byer at first enjoyed soccer. He played and became a professional. Eventually he switched over to technical skills and realized that was where his passion lay. He never tried to coach a club or work within a rigid soccer organization. His goal was always clear: to change an entire generation of players from the bottom up.

We have to see what we hope to achieve, but we must have a clear goal. At different points we may come to realize that we are not sure where we are going. Then out of nowhere a new order appears and the path becomes clear. In his book *Old Masters and Young Prodigies*, Paul Galenson shows how two different types of artists exist. Young prodigies often paint by instinct. Galenson considers Picasso a prodigy—for prodigies, things just happen. Old masters are not that "talented." He presents the opposite example in Cézanne, who had little "talent" and basically kept drawing and painting until he gained mastery. Some of us will have things that come easily at which we can excel at an early age. As time goes by we may also begin to branch out in new directions. With every cycle, it is important to observe and not lose clarity. The world is a complicated place and humans are complicated beings. In this minefield of potential future achievements, clarity can help keep us on the right course. Put everything aside and try to look clearly at the path you are taking. Don Juan might suggest that, like Carlos Castañeda, we should learn to pursue our goals with passion, clarity, and purpose.

BIBLIOGRAPHY

CHAPTER 1

Chase, W. G., & Simon, H. A. (1973a). The mind's eye in chess. In W. G. Chase (Ed.), *Visual information processing* (pp. 215–281). Academic Press.

Chase, W. G., & Simon, H. A. (1973b). Perception in chess. *Cognitive Psychology*, *4*, 55–81.

De Groot, A. (1978). *Thought and choice in chess*. Mouton.

Ericsson, A., & Pool, R. (2017). *Peak: Secrets from the new science of expertise*. Houghton Mifflin Harcourt.

Flege, J. E. (2018). It's input that matters most, not age. *Bilingualism: Language and Cognition*, *21*(5), 919–920. https://doi.org/10.1017/S136672891800010X

Gladwell, M. (2008). *Outliers: The story of success*. Little, Brown and Co.

Hernandez, A. E. (2013). *The bilingual brain*. Oxford University Press.

Hernandez, A. E., & Li, P. (2007). Age of acquisition: Its neural and computational mechanisms. *Psychological Bulletin*, *133*(4), 638–650. https://doi.org/10.1037/0033-2909.133.4.638

Hu, Y., Ericsson, K. A., Yang, D., & Lu, C. (2009). Superior self-paced memorization of digits in spite of a normal digit span: The structure of a memorist's skill. *Journal of Experimental Psychology: Learning, Memory, and Cognition, 35*(6), 1426–1442. https://doi.org/10.1037/a0017395

Humpstone, H. J. (1919). Memory span tests. *The Psychological Clinic, 12*, 196–200.

Martin, P. R., & Fernberger, S. W. (1929). Improvement in memory span. *The American Journal of Psychology, 41*(1), 91–94. https://doi.org/10.2307/1415112

Reiterer, S. M. (2019). Neuro-psycho-cognitive markers for pronunciation/speech imitation as language aptitude. In Z. Wen, P. Skehan, A. Biedroń, S. Li, & S. L. Sparks (Eds.), *Language aptitude: Advancing theory, testing, research and practice* (pp. 277–299). Taylor & Francis.

Schraw, G. (2005). An interview with K Anders Ericsson. *Educational Psychology Review, 17*(4), 389–412. https://doi.org/10.1007/s10648-005-8139-0

CHAPTER 2

Bjork, R. A., & Benjamin, A. S. (2011). On the symbiosis of remembering, forgetting, and learning. In A. S. Benjamin (Ed.), *Successful remembering and successful forgetting: A festschrift in honor of Robert A. Bjork* (pp. 1–22). Psychology Press.

Epstein, D. J. (2019). *Range: Why generalists triumph in a specialized world*. Riverhead Books.

McLaughlin, D. (2014). *The first half of a journey in human potential: Halfway to the 10,000 hour goal, four years of a blog by Dan McLaughlin (the Dan Plan book 1)*. Retrieved from Amazon.com.

CHAPTER 3

Bilbo, S., & Stevens, B. (2017). Microglia: The brain's first responders. *Cerebrum, 2017*. https://www.ncbi.nlm.nih.gov/pubmed/30210663

Capaldi, N. (2004). *John Stuart Mill: A biography*. Cambridge University Press.

Hiyoshi, A., Miyahara, K., Kato, C., & Ohshima, Y. (2011). Does a DNA-less cellular organism exist on Earth? *Genes Cells*, *16*(12), 1146–1158. https://doi.org/10.1111/j.1365-2443.2011.01558.x

Mill, J. S., Robson, J. M., McRae, R. F., (1974). *Collected works of John Stuart Mill. 7, 7*. University of Toronto Press; Routledge & Kegan Paul.

Ramón y Cajal, S. (1937). *Recuerdos de mi vida*. MIT Press.

Sierra, A., de Castro, F., Del Río-Hortega, J., Rafael Iglesias-Rozas, J., Garrosa, M., & Kettenmann, H. (2016). The "Big-Bang" for modern glial biology: Translation and comments on Pío del Río-Hortega 1919 series of papers on microglia. *Glia*, *64*(11), 1801–1840. https://doi.org/10.1002/glia.23046

CHAPTER 4

Gordon, B. J., & Dapena, J. (2006). Contributions of joint rotations to racquet speed in the tennis serve. *Journal of Sports Sciences*, *24*(1), 31–49. https://doi.org/10.1080/02640410400022045

Yandell, J. (1990). *Visual tennis: Mental imagery and the quest for the winning edge*. Doubleday.

CHAPTER 5

De Vries, R. (1969). Constancy of generic identity in the years three to six. *Monographs of the Society for Research in Child Development*, *34*(3), iii–67. https://doi.org/10.2307/1165683

Duranton, G., & Turner, M. A. (2011). The fundamental law of road congestion: Evidence from US cities. *American Economic Review*, *101*(6), 2616–2652. https://doi.org/10.1257/aer.101.6.2616

Fiebach, C. J., Friederici, A. D., Muller, K., von Cramon, D. Y., & Hernandez, A. E. (2003). Distinct brain representations for early and late learned words. *Neuroimage*, *19*(4), 1627–1637. http://www.ncbi.nlm.nih.gov/entrez/query.fcgi?cmd=Retrieve&db=PubMed&dopt=Citation&list_uids=12948717

Long, X., Benischek, A., Dewey, D., & Lebel, C. (2017). Age-related functional brain changes in young children. *Neuroimage*, *155*, 322–330. https://doi.org/https://doi.org/10.1016/j.neuroimage.2017.04.059

Lorch, M. P. (2009). History of aphasia: Multiple languages, memory, and regression: An examination of Ribot's Law. *Aphasiology*, *23*(5), 643–654. https://doi.org/https://doi.org/10.1080/02687030801931182

Ribot, T. A. (1881). *Les maladies de la mémoire* (2nd ed.). Ballière.

Ribot, T. A. (1882). *Diseases of memory: An essay in the positive psychology*. D. Appleton.

Woods, E. A., Hernandez, A. E., Wagner, V. E., & Beilock, S. L. (2014). Expert athletes activate somatosensory and motor planning regions of the brain when passively listening to familiar sports sounds. *Brain and Cognition*, *87*, 122–133. https://doi.org/https://doi.org/10.1016/j.bandc.2014.03.007

CHAPTER 6

Byer, T. (2016). Soccer Starts at Home. T3.

Ratey, J. J., & Hagerman, E. (2008). *Spark: The revolutionary new science of exercise and the brain*. Little, Brown.

Tepolt, F. A., Feldman, L., & Kocher, M. S. (2018). Trends in pediatric ACL reconstruction from the PHIS database. *Journal of Pediatric Orthopaedics*, *38*(9), e490–e494. https://doi.org/10.1097/bpo.0000000000001222

CHAPTER 7

Brigandt, I. (2005). The instinct concept of the early Konrad Lorenz. *Journal of the History of Biology*, *38*(3), 571–608. https://doi.org/http://dx.doi.org/10.1007/s10739-005-6544-3

Dehaene, S., & Cohen, L. (2007). Cultural recycling of cortical maps. *Neuron*, *56*(2), 384–398. https://doi.org/10.1016/j.neuron.2007.10.004

Dehaene, S., & Cohen, L. (2011). The unique role of the visual word form area in reading. *Trends in Cognitive Sciences, 15*(6), 254–262. https://doi.org/https://doi.org/10.1016/j.tics.2011.04.003

Desimone, R., Albright, T. D., Gross, C. G., & Bruce, C. (1984). Stimulus-selective properties of inferior temporal neurons in the macaque. *The Journal of Neuroscience, 4*(8), 2051. https://doi.org/10.1523/JNEUROSCI.04-08-02051.1984

Epstein, D. J. (2014). *The sports gene: Inside the science of extraordinary athletic performance.* New York, Current.

Gauthier, I. (1998). *Dissecting face recognition: The role of categorization level and expertise in visual object recognition* (Publication No. 9831438) [Doctoral Dissertation, Yale University]. ProQuest Dissertations & Theses Global. http://search.proquest.com.ezproxy.lib.uh.edu/docview/304460239?accountid=7107

Goren, C. C., Sarty, M., & Wu, P. Y. K. (1975). Visual following and pattern discrimination of face-like stimuli by newborn infants. *Pediatrics, 56*(4), 544. http://pediatrics.aappublications.org/content/56/4/544.abstract

Haxby, J. V., Horwitz, B., Ungerleider, L. G., Maisog, J. M., Pietrini, P., & Grady, C. L. (1994). The functional organization of human extrastriate cortex: A PET-rCBF study of selective attention to faces and locations. *The Journal of Neuroscience, 14*(11), 6336. https://doi.org/10.1523/JNEUROSCI.14-11-06336.1994

Johnson, M. H., Griffin, R., Csibra, G., Halit, H., Farroni, T., de Haan, M., Tucker, L. A., Baron-Cohen, S., & Richards, J. (2005). The emergence of the social brain network: Evidence from typical and atypical development. *Development and Psychopathology, 17*(3), 599–619. https://doi.org/10.1017/S0954579405050297

Kanwisher, N. (2017). The quest for the FFA and where it led. *The Journal of Neuroscience, 37*(5), 1056. https://doi.org/10.1523/JNEUROSCI.1706-16.2016

Kosakowski, H., Cohen, M., Takahashi, A., Keil, B., Kanwisher, N., & Saxe, R. (2022). Selective responses to faces, scenes, and bodies in the ventral visual pathway of infants. *Current Biology: CB, 32*(2), 265–274.e5. https://doi.org/10.1016/j.cub.2021.10.064

Lorenz, K. (1935). Der Kumpan in der Umwelt des Vogels. Der Artgenosse als auslösendes Moment sozialer Verhaltungsweisen. [The companion in the bird's world. The fellow-member of the species as releasing factor of social behavior.] *Journal für Ornithologie. Beiblatt. (Leipzig)*, 83, 137–213. https://doi.org/10.1007/BF01905355

Morton, J., & Johnson, M. H. (1991). CONSPEC and CONLERN: A two-process theory of infant face recognition. *Psychological Review*, 98(2), 164–181. https://doi.org/10.1037/0033-295x.98.2.164

Pieh, C., Proudlock, F., & Gottlob, I. (2012). Smooth pursuit in infants: Maturation and the influence of stimulation. *British Journal of Ophthalmology*, 96(1), 73. https://doi.org/10.1136/bjo.2010.191726

Sergent, J., Ohta, S., & MacDonald, B. (1992). Functional neuroanatomy of face and object processing: A positron emission tomography study. *Brain*, 115(1), 15–36. https://doi.org/10.1093/brain/115.1.15

Simion, F., Regolin, L., & Bulf, H. (2008). A predisposition for biological motion in the newborn baby. *Proceedings of the National Academy of Sciences*, 105(2), 809. https://doi.org/10.1073/pnas.0707021105

Tiffin-Richards, S. P., & Schroeder, S. (2020). Context facilitation in text reading: A study of children's eye movements. *Journal of Experimental Psychology: Learning, Memory, and Cognition*, 46(9), 1701–1713. https://doi.org/10.1037/xlm0000834

Tinbergen, N. (1989). *The study of instinct*. Clarendon.

Vallortigara, G., & Versace, E. (2018). Filial imprinting. In J. Vonk & T. Shackelford (Eds.), *Encyclopedia of animal cognition and behavior* (pp. 1–4). Springer International Publishing. https://doi.org/10.1007/978-3-319-47829-6_1989-1

von Hofsten, C., & Rosander, K. (2018). The development of sensorimotor intelligence in infants. In *Studying the perception-action system as a model system for understanding development* (pp. 73–106). Elsevier Academic Press. https://doi.org/10.1016/bs.acdb.2018.04.003

Whiteside, D., Martini, D. N., Zernicke, R. F., & Goulet, G. C. (2016). Ball speed and release consistency predict pitching success in Major League Baseball. *The Journal of Strength & Conditioning Research*, 30(7). https://journals.lww.com/nsca-jscr/Fulltext/2016/07000/Ball_Speed_and_Release_Consistency_Predict.1.aspx

Xu, Y. (2005). Revisiting the role of the fusiform face area in visual expertise. *Cerebral Cortex*, 15(8), 1234–1242. https://doi.org/10.1093/cercor/bhi006

CHAPTER 8

Goodall, J., & Berman, P. L. (2005). *Reason for hope: A spiritual journey.* Warner.

CHAPTER 9

Abukhalaf, A. H. I. (2021). The impact of Linguistic Monopoly on research quality in academic fields. *Academia Letters.* https://doi.org /https://doi.org/10.20935/AL3493

Archila-Suerte, P., Zevin, J., Bunta, F., & Hernandez, A. E. (2012). Age of acquisition and proficiency in a second language independently influence the perception of non-native speech. *Bilingualism: Language and Cognition, 15*(1), 190–201. https://doi.org/10.1017/S1366728911 000125

Conrad, J. (2007). *Heart of darkness* (R. H. O. Knowles, Ed.). Penguin Classics.

Defoe, D. (2012). *Robinson Crusoe.* Penguin Classics.

Demuth, K., Patrolia, M., Song, J. Y., & Masapollo, M. (2012). The development of articles in children's early Spanish: Prosodic interactions between lexical and grammatical form. *First Language, 32*(1–2), 17–37. https://doi.org/10.1177/0142723710396796

Erard, M. (2014). *Babel no more: The search for the world's most extraordinary language learners.* New York: Free Press.

Hernandez, A. E., Ronderos, J., Bodet, J. P., Claussenius-Kalman, H., Nguyen, M. V. H., & Bunta, F. (2021). German in childhood and Latin in adolescence: On the bidialectal nature of lexical access in English. *Humanities and Social Sciences Communications, 8*(1), 162. https:// doi.org/10.1057/s41599-021-00836-4

Kuhl, P. K. (2004). Early language acquisition: Cracking the speech code. *Nature Reviews Neuroscience, 5*(11), 831–841. http://www.nature.com/

Kuhl, P. K., Tsao, F. M., & Liu, H. M. (2003). Foreign-language experience in infancy: Effects of short-term exposure and social interaction on phonetic learning. *Proceedings of the National Academy of Sciences of the United States of America, 100*(15), 9096–9101. http://www.ncbi

.nlm.nih.gov/entrez/query.fcgi?cmd=Retrieve&db=PubMed&dopt=Citation&list_uids=12861072

Lieberman, E., Michel, J.-B., Jackson, J., Tang, T., & Nowak, M. A. (2007). Quantifying the evolutionary dynamics of language. *Nature*, *449*(7163), 713–716. https://doi.org/10.1038/nature06137

Morgan, J. L., & Demuth, K. (1996). Signal to syntax: An overview. In J. L. Morgan & K. Demuth (Eds.), *Signal to syntax: Bootstrapping from speech to grammar in early acquisition* (pp. 1–22). Lawrence Erlbaum Associates.

Morgan, J. L., & Demuth, K. (Eds.). (1996). *Signal to syntax: Bootstrapping from speech to grammar in early acquisition*. Lawrence Erlbaum Associates.

Pinker, S. (1994). *The language instinct*. William Morrow.

Reali, F., Chater, N., & Christiansen, M. H. (2018). Simpler grammar, larger vocabulary: How population size affects language. *Proceedings of the Royal Society B: Biological Sciences*, *285*(1871), 20172586. https://doi.org/10.1098/rspb.2017.2586

Reiterer, S. M. (2019). Neuro-psycho-cognitive markers for pronunciation/speech imitation as language aptitude. In Z. Wen, P. Skehan, A. Biedroń, S. Li, & S. L. Sparks (Eds.), *Language aptitude: Advancing theory, testing, research and practice* (pp. 277–299). Taylor & Francis.

Turker, S., & Reiterer, S. M. (2021). Brain, musicality and language aptitude: A complex interplay. *Annual Review of Applied Linguistics*, 1–13. https://doi.org/10.1017/S0267190520000148

Werker, J. F., & Tees, R. C. (2005). Speech perception as a window for understanding plasticity and commitment in language systems of the brain. *Developmental Psychobiology*, *46*(3), 233–234. http://www.wiley.com/WileyCDA/

CHAPTER 10

Grosser, M., Schonborn, R., & Hansen, U. (2002). *Competitive tennis for young players: The road to becoming a top player*. Meyer & Meyer Verlag.

Váša, F., Romero-Garcia, R., Kitzbichler, M. G., Seidlitz, J., Whitaker, K. J., Vaghi, M. M., Kundu, P., Patel, A. X., Fonagy, P., Dolan, R. J.,

Jones, P. B., Goodyer, I. M., Vértes, P. E., & Bullmore, E. T. (2020). Conservative and disruptive modes of adolescent change in human brain functional connectivity. *Proceedings of the National Academy of Sciences, 117*(6), 3248. https://doi.org/10.1073/pnas.1906144117

CHAPTER 11

Burkhardt, R. W., Jr. (2013). Lamarck, evolution, and the inheritance of acquired characters. *Genetics, 194*(4), 793–805. https://doi.org/10.1534/genetics.113.151852

Cole, T. J., & Mori, H. (2018). Fifty years of child height and weight in Japan and South Korea: Contrasting secular trend patterns analyzed by SITAR. *American Journal of Human Biology, 30*(1), e23054. https://doi.org/https://doi.org/10.1002/ajhb.23054

Darwin, C., & Kebler, L. (1859). *On the origin of species by means of natural selection, or, The preservation of favoured races in the struggle for life.* J. Murray. http://hdl.loc.gov/loc.rbc/General.17473.1

Elman, J. L. (1996). *Rethinking innateness: A connectionist perspective on development.* MIT Press.

Epstein, D. J. (2014). *The sports gene: Inside the science of extraordinary athletic performance.* New York, Current.

Gopnik, M., & Crago, M. B. (1991). Familial aggregation of a developmental language disorder. *Cognition, 39*(1), 1–50. https://doi.org/10.1016/0010-0277(91)90058-c

Harden, K. P. (2021). *The genetic lottery: Why DNA matters for social equality.* Princeton University Press.

Macnamara, B. N., Hambrick, D. Z., & Oswald, F. L. (2014). Deliberate practice and performance in music, games, sports, education, and professions: a meta-analysis. *Psychological Science, 25*(8), 1608–1618. https://doi.org/10.1177/0956797614535810

Pinker, S. (1994). *The language instinct.* William Morrow.

Waddington, C. H. (1957). *The strategy of the genes; a discussion of some aspects of theoretical biology.* Allen & Unwin.

Weismann, A., Parker, W. N., & Rönnfeldt, H. (1893). *The germ-plasm: A theory of heredity.* C. Scribner's Sons.

CHAPTER 12

Demick, B. (2019, August. 8). One is Chinese. One is American. How a journalist discovered and reunited identical twins. *Los Angeles Times*.

Demick, B. (2009, September 20). A young girl pines for her twin. *Los Angeles Times*.

Konigsberg, E. (2009, August 24). Unseparated since birth. *New York Times Magazine*.

CHAPTER 13

Basten, U., & Fiebach, C. J. (2021). Functional brain imaging of intelligence. In A. K. Barbey, R. J. Haier, & S. Karama (Eds.), *The Cambridge handbook of intelligence and cognitive neuroscience* (pp. 235–260). Cambridge University Press. https://doi.org/DOI: 10.1017/9781108635462.016

Beilock, S. (2010). *Choke: What the secrets of the brain reveal about getting it right when you have to*. Free Press.

Jeon, H.-A., & Friederici, A. D. (2017). What does "being an expert" mean to the brain? Functional specificity and connectivity in expertise. *Cerebral Cortex, 27*(12), 5603–5615. https://doi.org/10.1093/cercor/bhw329

Johnson, M. (2011). Face perception: A developmental perspective. In A. Calder, G. Rhodes, M. Johnson, & J. Haxby (Eds.), *Oxford Handbook of Face Perception* (pp. 3–14). Oxford University Press.

Slutter, M. W. J., Thammasan, N., & Poel, M. (2021). Exploring the brain activity related to missing penalty kicks: An fNIRS study [Original Research]. *Frontiers in Computer Science, 3*(32). https://doi.org/10.3389/fcomp.2021.661466

Weiskrantz, L. (1990). *Blindsight: A case study and implications*. Clarendon.

CHAPTER 14

Dickens, W. T., & Flynn, J. R. (2001). Heritability estimates versus large environmental effects: The IQ paradox resolved. *Psychological Review, 108*(2), 346–369. https://doi.org/10.1037/0033-295X.108.2.346

Flynn, J. R. (1980). *Race, IQ, and Jensen*. Routledge & Kegan Paul.

Jensen, A. R. (1972). *Genetics and education*. Harper & Row.

Shuey, A. M. (1966). *The testing of Negro intelligence*. Social Science Press.

Trahan, L. H., Stuebing, K. K., Fletcher, J. M., & Hiscock, M. (2014). The Flynn effect: A meta-analysis. *Psychological Bulletin, 140*(5), 1332–1360. https://doi.org/10.1037/a0037173

CHAPTER 15

Barabási, A.-L. (2018). *The formula: The universal laws of success*. Little, Brown and Company.

Beard, K. S. (2015). Theoretically speaking: An interview with Mihaly Csikszentmihalyi on flow theory development and its usefulness in addressing contemporary challenges in education. *Educational Psychology Review, 27*(2), 353–364. https://doi.org/10.1007/s10648-014-9291-1

Frankl, V. E. (2004). *Man's search for meaning: The classic tribute to hope from the Holocaust*. Rider.

Frankl, V. E. (2010). . . . *trotzdem Ja zum Leben sagen: Ein Psychologe erlebt das Konzentrationslager*. Kösel-Verlag.

CHAPTER 16

Beasley, J. (2021, June 30). 20 years ago he was in immigration purgatory. Now he's one of the fastest 40-somethings alive. *Runner's World*. https://www.runnersworld.com/runners-stories/a30897686/memo-morales-mexican-immigrant-marathon-runner/

Castaneda, C. (1998). *The teachings of Don Juan: A Yaqui way of knowledge. Deluxe 30th anniversary ed. with a new author commentary*. University of California Press.

CONCLUSION

Galenson, D. W. (2006). *Old masters and young geniuses: The two life cycles of artistic creativity*. Princeton University Press.

Lewis, M. (2000). *The new new thing: A Silicon Valley story*. W. W. Norton.

INDEX

Page numbers in italics refer to figures.

INDEX   **215**

emergent phenomena, 23
English language, vii; British, 107;
    as dominant language, 105–6,
    109; emergence and, 111–12;
    French language and, 111;
    German language and, x, xi,
    106–12; Latin language and,
    107–12; learning, 3, 102, 107–9,
    112, 158; as lingua franca, 105;
    as simplified, 106, 110
English speakers, ix, 102, 105,
    110, 112
Enrique, Luis, 59
environment: development and,
    135–38; individual ability and,
    128–29, 168; IQ and, 170–72,
    186; physical tasks, mental tasks
    and, 163. *See also* genetics,
    environment and
epigenetics, 135–40, 143
Epstein, David, 21, 83, 138, 139
Erard, Michael, 99, 101
Ericsson, K. Anders, 12, 14, 65,
    129, 150; deliberate practice
    approach of, 1–5, 13, 15,
    17, 20, 36, 40, 128, 151,
    176–78; digit span research
    of, 9–11; golf expertise and,
    16–17; McLaughlin and, 15–17;
    mental representation and, 5;
    Peak, 5
Esther, 146–48
Euwe, Max, 6
evolution, 24–25, 54
expertise: age of skill acquisition
    and, 12; aptitude and, 7; FFA
    and, 87; golf, 15–21, 67, 141;

memory and, 5–8; research
    on, 5–8; visual, 86–87. *See also*
    specific topics
experts: adults becoming, 15–21,
    159; brain and, 159; choking
    and, 159, 160; dog, 86–87;
    mental representations in, 5.
    See also specific topics
eyes: blindsight, 156; eyesight,
    82–83; fixations, 84; motion
    tracking, 79–84

face processing: brain and face
    tracking, 79–80, 86–88, 98; face
    blindness, 93; face recognition,
    93, 95, 99; FFA and, 85–87, 88;
    infant, 86, 88, 98; research on,
    78–80, 85–87; tracking faces,
    78–81, 86, 87, 98, 178; visual
    expertise and, 86–87
Farsi, vii, ix, xi, 132
Federer, Roger, 166, 167, 168,
    196
Feldman, Lanna, 66
Fernberger, S. W., 8–9
fetus movement, 80
FFA. *See* fusiform face area
Fiebach, Christian, 53, 56, 160
filial imprinting, 76
Finch, Jenny, 83
flattening, 36
flexibilidad principle of mastery,
    192, 195–96
flow, 176, 187
Flynn, James, 169, 170, 171–72,
    186
Flynn Effect, 169